HABITS OF A
CHAMPION

NOBODY BECOMES A CHAMPION BY ACCIDENT
#HABITSOFACHAMPION

15 LESSONS OF SUCCESS BY FORMER
NEW YORK YANKEES PERFORMANCE
COACH, DANA CAVALEA

Hardback ISBN: 978-1-64184-953-1
Paperback ISBN: 978-1-64184-038-5
Ebook ISBN: 978-1-64184-954-8

Contents

To all those future Champions out there. Becoming a Champion begins with a decision. A decision followed by great habits, A clear mission, and the desire to make magic happen. Lead with a purpose.

Always remember, championships start with you. All-in.

Foreword

I have been privileged and blessed to experience what it is like to become a World Champion, both as a player, and as a manager.

I have been asked which I value more, and to that question, my answer is always the same.

"I love to win. I love to compete. Winning as a player took immense amounts of work, sacrifice, discipline, and commitment. Winning as a manager took immense amount of work, sacrifice, discipline, and commitment."

The lesson here is that winning takes work. Not just work for the sake of working. Planned, calculated, detail-oriented work. As a player, I worked very diligently to stay in the Majors. Every year, new talent came into the game, some of whom were looking to take my position. I always leaned on my work ethic for not only strength and confidence, but for survival.

Major League Baseball is a competitive place. If you sit back, take the easy way out, and expect nobody will take your job, you are mistaken.

As a player, I learned to play through pain, encouraged teammates who were struggling, and learned how to deal with the day to day failures that come with the sport of baseball.

It was not easy. In order to get through "the grind," you rely heavily on your faith, your family, and your daily habits and routines.

When the waters get rough, you find stability and comfort in your daily routines.

As a player, you have routines that include strength training, conditioning, mental conditioning, nutritional planning, as well as skill training such as hitting, throwing, and defensive work. All are important and require daily attention.

As a catcher, I worried not only about myself, but also about that pitcher that stood sixty feet-six inches away from me each night. Did he have his A-Game tonight or was he struggling right out of the gate? Either way, we were going to struggle together or sail smoothly together. I embraced whatever came my way.

My habits and routines gave me the fortitude I needed to keep going.

Habits and routines also kept things in order for me, so I could find a balance between my professional life and personal life. When you have a routine, you know what time you leave for the park each day. You know when you are focusing on your personal health and fitness. You know what you are eating for breakfast, lunch, and dinner.

Routines provide structure. When you combine discipline and structure with solid habits and routines, your chances of winning and having success improve greatly.

As my journeyman career went from player to manager, I realized how many players struggled to find solid routines and habits to keep them grounded. It was my job as a manager to help develop players, which meant introducing them to routines that could help them improve their chances for success.

It was my job to show players I cared about them. I always made sure to lead with my heart and managed the game based on my gut instincts alongside my daily notes derived from hours of preparation.

In order to win, you must have great habits, routines, and buy-in to your process. But there is something above all of these things that can take you to places you only dream of.

Passion.

What I am most passionate about is the game of baseball, getting the most out of my players, and the daily competition that leads to winning.

Passion is the one thing that can make up for deficits that you may have in your plan. No matter how much time you spend on your plan, it may not be perfect. Your passion though, is what keeps you fighting for excellence every single day.

When you combine passion with discipline, work-ethic, a great plan, and solid routines, your chances of becoming a Champion not only on the field, but in life, goes way up.

Look to become a Champion in all that you do. Lead with your heart. Become a Champion in life and always remember your passion when times get tough.

If you honor that passion, you will always end up on the other side of all obstacles that stand between you and your goals.

Now go out and win today!

Joe Girardi,
MLB Network Host, MLB World Series
Champion Manager, former MLB Player

Introduction

I wrote this book with one purpose: To share with you some of the people, lessons, and experiences that have shaped me into who I am today hoping they can do the same for you and those you lead, taking you from where you are today and forming the *Habits of a Champion* in all areas of your life.

These fifteen lessons have given me strength when I needed it, power when I didn't have it, and, most importantly, the guts to overcome the fears I face every single day. I wrote this book for each of you who embodies the person I am today: the athlete, the coach, the businessman, the entrepreneur, the husband, the father, and the rebellious dreamer who may have lost his way once or twice but refused to quit.

Read with an open mind; skip chapters if you like as they are in no particular order. Someone once told me that your "life" should turn like the pages in a book, one after the other, one chapter after the next, but I never agreed with that way of being

I don't really like *order* so I decided to write a book that you can pick up wherever you desire. Kind of like the way I view life; There are no rules. Be a renegade. Challenge the status quo. Inspire those around you. And, always have fun!

Much like you, I struggle to balance life and time. I battle with myself and my emotions every day. I'm challenged by the constant balance between acknowledging prior accomplishments and contentment with who I am today, along with the pursuit of excellence, satisfaction with my current state, and the constant desire for more in all categories of my life. The addiction of success in a world that no longer asks for it, but demands it.

How much is enough? A question I ask myself almost daily.

When will I know I have made it? Another daily ask.

How can I achieve more while still having a personal life, leverage over my career, and a family that is getting my focused attention, while still keeping my youthful, dreamer spirit?

These are the questions I ask myself.

I've gotten lost several times along my journey as I copied the habits, words, and actions of others until it felt so wrong I had to stop. Other times, I forgot who I was, what I enjoyed in life, my preferences versus my dislikes. It made me sick. Sick in a way no doctor could understand. Emotionally sick. Sick of the noise in my head. The thoughts of others, posing as my own, every conscious minute of the day. Sick with stress. Sick with anxiety. Sick with fear. Sick of my constant lack of focus. Sick of my desire to be constantly looking at the highlight reels of others. The good old comparison game. The game where the one who decides to compare their life to that of others, always ends up the loser.

I had no idea why somebody with *all the tools* had to go through this self inflicted hell. After all, I am the Coach. The Coach can't break. I've dedicated my life, my *job and career* to serving others and helping them to overcome their greatest obstacles. Now how would I overcome mine? How could this have happened to me?

Then I realized *why*. That magical "why" that everybody speaks of these days. Alongside coaching, my other passions in life include speaking, writing, and motivating others to *greatness*. I believe I'm commissioned by the powers above to suffer in order to reflect, learn, and then apply all the lessons to continue my journey and lifetime quest of helping others. I will accomplish that commissioned "why" by writing this book and going on the speaking tour that will accompany it. My experiences are meant to drive me forward by first pulling me back.

Once I realized that I was not the victim of my circumstances, but the beneficiary, my game changed. So can yours.

When I truly understood my path of pain and what it meant, I couldn't shake the repetitive feeling in my gut that said: Write it and tell it. Write about my struggles. Tell my story. Inspire and motivate others through their journey to greatness. Inspire their Championship life and journey. Inspire them to spread their message. To live their champion life with passion, joy, and conviction.

That is what brings me to this point today. This book is my passion. This book is my life story in fifteen short chapters designed to show you that even the toughest competitors can break and rebuild.

The toughest people can get lost, lose their faith, their swagger, and regain their path.

Resilience, Guts, & Grit. vs. Fear, Scarcity, and Loss.

For many years, I thought one side of the above equation had to beat the other. And, it can happen. But, what I came to realize is that there will always be this battle between the two sides of that equation— the battle between good (resilience, guts, grit) and evil (fear, scarcity, loss) you could say.

It is about acknowledging the power of each side, respecting it, then moving forward with unshakable determination toward your goals and dreams.

As I wrote this book, I was able to relive my circumstances, conversations, experiences, and defining moments. In doing so, I realized one thing; I can handle anything that comes my way.

One of my favorite conversations comes from a special lady in my life, Anita. She is ninety years old and changed my perspective in an instant when she told me *life doesn't get easier, it only gets harder*. So, go get better. Get good at dealing with yourself. Master your mind.

You see, Coaches have coaches too. They come in all ages and life experience levels.

Your mindset is everything. When your world feels like it is crumbling, remember, it is only happening in your own mind. If you are down on your luck, it's only in your own mind. And if you feel like the world is on your shoulders, that things won't improve, that you are stuck and can't see a way out, remember, it is all in your mind.

You have the power to change your mindset in an instant. Do it. Never sulk.

Becoming a Champion results from all the hardships you face in a day, week, month, year—your entire lifetime. In the end, if you are still standing with some money to your name, character, integrity, reputation intact, and have built a legacy based on helping others win, you have succeeded.

I hope these stories inspire you and motivate you to see life from the batter's box where every pitch is a fastball down the middle, and you have A-Rod's swing. There will be pitches you should watch go by you. But remember, always be swinging.

Swing hard, you may just hit one out of the park.

To the Champion in all of us,
Coach Dana Cavalea

ONE

You Gotta Hate to Lose More than You Love to Win

How do you know if somebody will be a valuable asset for your team? A real go-getter. A blue-blooded winner. Outside of their overall self-proclaimed results and track record, which anyone can fudge on a resume and brotherly reference list, asking a simple question will help speed up your conclusion of the type of player you have trying out for your *team.*

Do you hate to lose... or love to win?

Although loving to win is great and much in line with the "everybody gets a trophy culture" of today, not wanting to lose shows that the person is the underdog with a chip on their shoulder and has a true willingness to do whatever it takes to win. I mean really, at the end of the day, *who doesn't love to win?*

What does it take to win? It takes grit and guts to win—the ability to get knocked around the school-yard. Most just don't *have "it"* on the surface. You know, the what "it" takes. They don't have the resilience to get knocked down and stand back up knowing the risk of getting knocked down again.

Finding somebody who actually sees some joy in the process of *defeat*, which is a key part of the winning process, is the person who is truly special when it comes right down to it. This is the person with the Champion pedigree.

Some have it naturally without trying. Some have it underneath layers of personal baggage. Some need it pulled out of them. Others don't have it at all and never will. It's a harsh reality, but the truth is the truth.

That is the only language to speak. The language of truth. I had a good friend of mine, Mark Zambrato, a New York City advertising executive, once tell me all you have is the truth. Everything that spills from your mouth should be from the side of truth. Anybody that ever says, *to tell you the truth* is a highly questionable person. What do they lie most of the time and in this instance they are shooting you straight? Gotta love the New York spirit. He's got a point.

Winning is not easy. Just ask any Champion or loser out there. They will all mention the day in and day out grind—the sleepless nights—the swelling in their gut and the clenched jaw while sleeping. The fear that takes over their bodies day after day. The disillusionment that hat dominates their mind.

Any winner out there, they are all extremely familiar with the few moments of glory that keeps them fighting for their next day. *How do you know if you have what it takes?*

Let me tell you one way. Research shows that those who actually "make-it" beyond their genetic talent, often come from a situation of hardship. A tough life. They come from homes where the daily struggle was evident. Many don't come from the best schools or universities. They don't come from homes of top investment bankers or attorneys. Their parents were not at the helm of fashion trends, rocking the newest Lululemon gear, Starbucks cup, Rolex watch or driving a Tesla. They come from average to below average people and homes in terms of character and income.

Many top performing "winners" in life, sports, and business came from underdog circumstances. The exact situation it takes to endure the unpredictable surprises of a winding road known as the *road to winning big*.

They struggled. They battled. Every single day. The fight was real and was about survival before it was about "making it."

This gives us all hope. It shows us we are not a product of our environment, but we can use our environment to motivate us to the top of our chosen discipline, whatever it may be. Environments can act as fuel rather than a ball and chain to accomplishment of our dreams.

One common trait I have seen among the winners I have worked with is that they have a deeply-rooted fear of "going back" to where they started or came from. They never want to experience "broke" ever again. The realities of their past forever plague them, keeping just enough healthy fear in their soul to never get lazy, never sit back, never coast, and certainly never quit; ever.

On the sports field, these types never want to take another minor league bus trip, sleep at the Days Inn, or eat peanut butter and jelly sandwiches as their nutrient-packed dinner. They want to be in the lineup every single day. They will play hurt. They will play tired. They will play sick. They need to be out there to meet their own expectations of excellence. Best of all, they will never complain.

The dark memories of their past keep them motivated for life. They keep these diehard *competitors* hungry. I mean really, after you eat filet mignon, do you want to eat hanger steak? Chances are, you have graduated from that peasant cuisine. You've earned it.

Becoming a Champion is about surviving the hardships of your youth as you fight day in and day out for your future. The fight never stops. The *knowing* is half the battle. It never gets easier, you get smarter (hopefully).

Taking the time to look within yourself and ask who is really inside is essential. Self-assessment, introspection and evaluation is a lost art. But remember, awareness is the key to change. *What do you find when you take the deep look inside yourself?*

Are you a junkyard dog, full of fight, or a sheep? The answer to this question will determine your aptitude for winning. Let's always remember that winning is black or white. I was fortunate enough to learn about winning from the great Derek Jeter. He would always say, *"You either win or you lose. That's it.*

If you don't win the World Series, you lost. It is really that simple. You lost."

It was that simple truth that helped me shape my view on what it takes to get to the front of the wolf pack.

Having a deep-down refusal to lose, the desire to always challenge yourself for a better performance, a commitment to instill your own winning values into those teammates around you, that is winning. That is how Champions think, act, behave, and believe. Even when the demand for personal excellence and the surrounding circumstances are not working or aligning in your favor.

What "DJ" also taught me was, defensiveness is masked insecurity, which reminds me of a personal story about dealing with The Captain.

On a cold September day in Detroit, Derek and I were in the athletic training room before a game. He was getting his ankles taped as I was getting dressed for the game. He asked me a question, and I snapped back at him. After he asked me why I was so defensive, he reminded me that defensiveness is just masked insecurity. The sad part was, I never realized I had a problem with defensiveness. Certainly not insecurity!

Coaching Tip: If you have high levels of defensiveness, you must address it. Take full responsibility, look deep within, understand the source, then self-correct via constant awareness and self-coaching. Realize how you interact with others; which situations make you engage or withdraw. See yourself from the outside in, then from the inside out. Sometimes, we are unaware of how we are behaving and that can allow us to go years without addressing our issues. Dangerous stuff man when left untreated.

I didn't believe it. I just could not wrap my head around my defensiveness and insecurity. But, over the years, I would realize he was 100 percent right. I had deep fears that I needed to address. He was the man that started the process of my breakthrough.

That is why he was The Captain. He knew how to get you. He knew how to win. He knew how to help others win. And, he always did it with class—never in public, and always at the perfect moment.

Remember this: *Not everybody is rooting for you.*

Something I realized in my years traveling with the Yankees was that as winners, there will always be those who root against us. Haters. Those who throw sticks into our path. Sometimes they may even wear the same uniform as you. They may even be from the same blood line. Possibly even a posing fan. But we must continue onward. What allows us the ability to trek through is that chip, our values, and our pride. Also, our families, coaches, and other support circles who unquestionably have our back. That circle may be small. Never leave them behind. Keep them first place. Those are your real fans. Always reward loyalty- it is the greatest human gift any leader can be given.

The Power of Pride.

Many in our world speak out against the word *pride*. But without pride, you have no standards or values. Pride is a defined value within us that allows us to either walk past a struggling friend or foe, or to step up and lead another baby cub (and future lion) to the promised land.

Pride can be bad when it is self-serving. But, pride is also embedded within the true essence of leadership. You cannot lead without pride. Every great leader has high levels of pride. They are proud of themselves. They are proud of how and who they lead. Their standards encourage others to be proud to don their colors. Pride is power.

Show me a real leader that is not proud. Show me a real leader who does not enter a room with conviction and presence. Show me a real leader who does not demand excellence from themselves and those he leads. You will not find it. Real leaders are winners. Real leaders make winners out of followers, but only if those followers choose to emulate the values of their Leader while still maintaining their own soul. The backbone and driving value of that leader is *pride*.

So, do you love to win or hate to lose?

That is the question. Do you choose to win at the expense of another teammate? If so, you have won, but that teammate and the team has lost. You showed the love for winning but paid no mind to losing the respect of your team and yourself.

What I appreciate about the question, *Do you love to win or hate to lose*, is that it makes you take inventory on who you are and what you stand for. Would you want to make one million dollars a year while the company is headed out of business?

How long will that million last as your severance? It is all interconnected. Teams cannot win if only the captain wins. Workforces cannot win if only the CEO wins. Both outcomes result from a bad culture.

In sports, the manager cannot overshadow the players. That results in resentment. It is all related. Everything matters.

In life, if you win and your friends and family struggle, what does that make you? A winner? Perhaps. But how good does it feel to watch those closest to you struggle? This does not suggest a hand-out, but rather encouragement rather than entitlement. With uncontrolled pride and loose lips many fortunes have been stripped through universal law.

One must never forget, the underdog spirit is one that we should never speak down on. That relentless pursuit to achieve and help others is an amazing gift. If you look around your current circle, you can always find that one friend who has the guts. You just know he or she will make it—do something special. Make the magic happen. That is the winner of the group. Minimal flash, but unshakable confidence. They have the "it" factor. They have the makeup to become a Champion in all they do.

Their purpose is far greater than themselves. It is as if they have a gift and they want to contribute to the world at a greater level than the average. They are willing to sacrifice themselves in a healthy way to make that happen.

Amazing. Their energy is infectious and contagious. When they come around, they share their gift of energy with everyone they come in contact with. Their infectious spirit can take you places you only dreamed of. It is your job to hold on for that ride, catch yourself up, and let their winning attitude drive you closer to success.

That is the spirit of the underdog. The Gift. The hating-to-lose attitude blended with a personal vision, mission, and goal. What if every team had the spirit of the underdog blended with a clear vision, mission, and goal? What would they be capable of?

I have always felt that if businesses ran their departments with the same values as a winning sports franchise, the results would be magical. Many have the nerve to compare their corporate organization to that of sports, but in all of my years as a corporate speaker and talent developer, I am yet to see it. In today's business climate, companies hire consultants for everything, including the delegation of leadership to outside consultants or specialists. Not good.

Can you imagine a sports team using an outside source to lead them to victory? It would be down right insane. When your team or organization is losing, the reality is, the wrong leadership is in place. The wrong culture is in place. The wrong team is in place. Because of that, production is down, earnings are down, and morale sucks. At that point you have what I like to call, "An unwinnable game."

Again, if this was the case with the sports team leadership, the manager would be sent packing. The under-performing players would be right behind him. And, anybody else that is not aligned with winning at this current moment. Winning happens in the present. There can be periods of redevelopment, restructuring, and retooling, but it must have a clear beginning, middle, and end. After that, if the results are not there, time to pull out the chainsaw.

The greatest part about sports is that everybody is on a short leash. Perform or be sent packing. Your stat line is your reality. Because of that culture, nobody takes their work for granted. There is a constant competitive pursuit to win. No complacency, just effort and appreciation for the office they hold. All parties involved know without victory comes loss. Personal and professional.

More spirit of the underdog and an absolute hatred to lose.

So, as you reflect on the question, "Do You Love to Win, or Hate to Lose?" think about the examples above why loving to win is based on a perfect world of fictional circumstance. Hate to Lose as if your life depends upon it. Because it does. Get present. Get real. Get winning.

TWO

Never Get Too High & Never Get Too Low.

Do you remember that buddy you used to play sports with who would lose his mind every time the game did not go their way? It was as if they were overtaken by an evil spirit when the tides shifted out of their favor.

We all know somebody like that. It can be a friend, family member, co-worker, or teammate that can melt down faster than an ice-cream cone on a hot summer day with the slightest hint of bad news. Even with good news, these people can get to levels of joy that are not even on the spectrum.

We usually play it off after years of watching these displays by saying, "Oh, that is just so-and-so. That's just how he/she is." They operate at the intersection of bipolar and manic-depressive, which are very real issues, but not an optimal diagnosis to have when somebody is seeking to optimize their performance.

Think about how exhausted you would be if your daily life was the equivalent of a soaring roller coaster at Universal Studios. Wicked highs followed by dramatic lows. Repeat. Repeat. Repeat. One can only hope for a few seconds of straight-away on the tracks to gather themselves for the next set of climbs and dips.

In all of my years watching top performers, behaviors like this were never present. Quite the opposite actually. It was almost as if the bigger the situation, the cooler their disposition. The bigger the deal on the table, the more chilled their veins became.

Which brings me to my next point. We're all fighting for the same physical resource and to keep that resource high in abundance. That resource is energy. Energy baby.

Gotta have it.

Energy is a word I always like to speak of since we only have so much of it each day. It is our job to respect, preserve, generate, and deploy that energy accordingly. You only get so much of it per day.

Coaching Tip: We must avoid people and situations that drain our energy, at all costs. The great Alex Rodriguez and author Jon Gordon refer to these people and situations as "darkness" or "energy vampires" and we must avoid them at all costs.

Watch out for those energy vampires. They will slow and cloud your thinking. They will alter your state of mind and being where decision making will become more emotional—less rational. Rational thought will be substituted for emotional impulse. Impulsive behavior is dangerous for the high performer.

What makes the energy vampire so lethal is these individuals are so poisonous, they will make you feel like you are in the wrong—the one with the problem. They see themselves as perfect, the victor, and you as the villain in every situation. Remember, snakes bite. Keep your distance. The greater the better. These individuals are also masters at gaining your trust over and over again with their charm and false radiance, but beware. They have repetitive patterns of biting once trust begins to climax. Guard yourself around this type.

Let's get real. We all know living a life among the negative is inevitable. Success amongst the negative comes down to your ability to act once they (the negative) are targeted and discovered. How quickly we can identify it (their negative traits, triggers, and behaviors), dispose of it (their negative traits, triggers, and behaviors), or redirect it (traits, triggers, and behaviors) determines our success in the battle against the negative, vampires. I call this The IDR Method. I made that up but let's go with it. Acronyms are *in* these days. Plus, it makes me sound like I am far more advanced in the behavioral sciences than I am.

What does the IDR Method do for us as high performers? The IDR method keeps us moving forward while navigating around potential hazards. It keeps toxic people away from us or at a healthy distance. Remember, darkness and vampires exist to serve themselves and take you down. The scary part is that they don't even know it. Their personal agenda is always the top priority. They live to serve themselves and their needs. You are often just a gateway to help them get to the place they believe will provide them with their life's *answers*. Watch out for self-serving generosity, over-gifting, and classic ups and downs in mood. These are all tell tale signs a vampire is in range.

One of my clients, a successful private equity titan, once told me, "Dana, there are three types of people in this world. The first is —a smart person. The second is, a bad person. The third is a stupid person. Do you know which is the most dangerous? I will tell you...

You see, the smart person you don't have to worry about. The bad person, you stay away from since you know what to expect. They're bad. But the stupid person, they're dangerous. They're unpredictable, they're impossible to negotiate with, and they're impossible to anticipate because even they don't know what their next move is, so how could you? These people are scary."

Coaching Tip: Stay away from stupid people. Protect your energy. How do you know somebody is "stupid"? They lack predictability, they're defensive, and they're unable to *work together*.

Let's talk about how people and situations can affect your internal psychology, which we all know is the starting point of performance optimization and Championship thoughts, behaviors, and actions.

Think about this question: *How many people and situations make you anxious?*

Probably more than you think! I call these internal highs and lows. Why is that?

Often, your internal centering system is off because you're unable to understand the behavior of others. Like a missile trying to hit a moving target. The missile sees the target, but since it keeps moving, the system has to keep recalibrating. Exhausting and can compromise accuracy even of the most sophisticated technology. The body and mind crave clarity and consistency in order to optimize performance.

So, rather than sticking around trying to understand the erratic behavior and thought process of a wild goose, get away from it and spend your energy elsewhere, or else you will be on a wild goose chase.

Do something positive. Spend your time where you can give and receive value. Yes, give. Never forget that receiving is often times the result of giving. Give as much as you can. It is the way to happiness, avoiding chronic depression—the "bad days". Show me somebody who is miserable and I will show you a selfish, narcissistic bastard.

Many of the clients I have worked with that suffered from mild depression and a self-diagnosed lack of purpose, really just stopped giving. The first step to getting them on track is getting them out of their own heads and back into a giving mode. Time and charitable donations of gifts and cash.

Now, let's talk about one of the greatest energy drains of our modern existence—social media. We need to get honest with each other. Do you actually feel good from spending hours per day staring at other people trying to showcase their personal high-light reel?

I get it. But, it's a temporary high, followed by longer term angst. "How could my life not be as good as theirs?" blah blah blah. More vampirism and energy deprivation. That's usually followed by you boosting yourself up with, "I am so much smarter, better looking, more educated." All protection for your battered ego and self-esteem.

More getting high. Then getting low.

But let me tell you this: the only reason most can post so much is because they are not working. They are not busy. Busy people do not have the time to spend taking and sharing pictures all day writing novels for captions. Social media has become a modern day digital bar or coffee shop where all the locals just "hang out" and share stories like the cast of Cheers or The Jersey Shore.

That is the real scoop. So put your phone down and get to work.

And just so you know, there will be people less qualified than you that succeed at a higher level than you in certain areas of life. Sometimes less-qualified leads to fearlessness. And fearlessness can get somebody ahead of the other 90 percent of the population who are too busy planning, contemplating, and talking themselves out of their own dreams (in their head, never taking action).

Energy draining goes way beyond just people.

You know, sometimes we think that it's just people and things that steal our energy, but our environment is also to blame. Have you ever walked into a room and have just felt amazing? The colors, the scents, everything is working. The mojo factor is high.

Well if you have experienced the high, I am sure you have experienced the low. The room that smells like three-year-old drunken urine, a litter box, beer bottles, and stale flatulence from a decaying couch. I know, a bit much, but I always find humor as a good way to lighten the mood, especially when it comes to personal development.

How do we overcome all of this? Let's get grounded. We all know a fast, racing mind is a dangerous mind. An overly excited mind, and an out of focus mind is ground zero for all hell to break loose. You know, the kind of mind looking for a clear target, but instead is acting more like a merry-go-round on amphetamines imported from Ibiza. That's a bad place to be—back on the roller coaster dip, preparing for a wicked up. It's the daily job of the true Champion to deploy strategies that quiet the noise.

But how? Meditation? Maybe. Deep Breathing? Yah. Hot Baths? Perhaps. Working Out? Definitely. Steam or Sauna? Yup. Massage? Anytime. Walking? That works.

All of these methods work. You need to find the ones that work best for you. Which methods fit who *you* are.

We are in the era of the guru. Meditation guru's say meditate. The yoga guru says lay in shavasana until mercury comes out of retrograde. Well, this is good for some, but not good for others.

I tried floating one time and ended up in the worst state of panic I have ever experienced. But wait, Stephen Curry does it. See what I mean? What works for one does not work for all. Stay in your lane. Do you.

That's what matters. I can suggest meditation, but if it's too voodoo witchcraft for you, we have no shot at consistency, which means, we have no shot at success. We lost in the locker room. You must be grounded, so whatever it takes to get you there is what you must do. Forget the fads, trends, and advice of influencers. Go on your own journey to discover "your way."

Honestly, could you imagine negotiating with somebody who can't focus? Or, somebody who isn't even listening to you as you're proposing terms to a huge deal? How about being married to somebody who spends most of their day in la-la land? (great movie, by the way- the chick flicks always get me).

What if that person is actually *you* and you're not even aware of it. The chances and margin for error go way up when you're anxious and not all there, or all here! Becoming fully present, even-keeled, and hyper-focused while maintaining a sense of calm and being collected is essential for Champion-like behavior and outcomes. As a member of some of the greatest Yankees teams ever, I was taught this important lesson.

Coaching Tip: Through good and bad, remain calm. Panic buttons create more panic. Fear causes us to push the panic button.

For example, on a hot summer night in 2009, we were playing a game in Atlanta against the Braves. We were on a ten-game losing streak and were called into the clubhouse for a team meeting by our General

Manager who happened to be on that trip. Cash (Brian Cashman) started off by saying, "This is not a meeting that is the result of panic. We just wanted to bring everybody together to get re-focused on the goal. The goal of winning."

Fortunately, since our meetings were frequent and commonplace, the team stepped up, gathered together, and went on to win the World Series that year. That meeting was a great turning point for us. It was the result of a GM having a great feel of his team and he knew not to press that panic button, but to address a current situation in a positive way.

This strategy works well when meeting is the standard and norm of the Organization and team. But, if meetings are not typical and are only being called when times are tough, that, my friends, is a "panic meeting." Panic meetings are dangerous and often result in hesitation, fear, timid play and defensive execution. The opposite emotions of what's needed to win. Don't push panic buttons, the results are usually the opposite of those that are desired.

I must say, after most of our team meetings, we would typically go out and win that night. I think the greatest benefits from our meetings was the sense of obligation and brotherhood that resulted from each meeting. We all got closer. That closeness and cama- raderie led to trust on the battlefield. We felt a sense of obligation to step up and win for each other. Win —for the organization. Winning was our priority. But the key to success is staying consistent and even tem- pered at all times. Set a standard way of operating, of winning, with consistent procedures and stick with them through thick and thin.

Mark Teixiera, a future Hall of Famer and a personal friend, once told me in the training room, while he was really struggling at the plate, "I am not doing great right now, but I keep working. I stick with my routine. I make minor adjustments, but I never change things completely because of my current result. Slumps are normal in baseball I just have to work through it and never doubt myself"

Or as Derek Jeter said, "The more I struggle, the more I don't hit, the closer I am to getting one." Simple words of genius that show true confidence and self-belief, in themselves and their routines.

Coaching Tip: Never get too high. Never get too low. Stay the course. A beautiful sunny day follows every storm.

So, remember, as emotional as life can be, ride the waves. Life has peaks, life has valleys. That is reality. Live in that reality at all times and the valleys won't surprise you. I've found that the key to life is to appreciate your peaks. Immerse yourself in the joy of them, always realizing you will have more valleys. It's all about how you handle things in your own mind. How are you handling the peaks and valleys? That is where true winning is done. True Champions are made between their own ears.

You want the edge on your competition? Train your mental state. Train to remain *calm*. Most people believe you are either born that way (calm and relaxed) or you are not. I believe everybody has a certain predisposition to being calm or getting nuts. That is truth. But, even if that is the case, you become more nuts if you give life to things that shouldn't be given life by applying your energy to those things.

Think about the room you are in right now. If I tell you to look for the color brown, I am sure you will find a lot of brown, or even colors that look like brown. Then, if I ask you how much red you saw, you probably didn't see any!

Why? You weren't focused on red. Get the point?

That negative person in the workplace can take down the entire work culture by bringing just a little bit of negativity, chatter, and gossip to work with them every day. They begin to mentally poison one person at a time. Then, that person tells another, and another, and before you know it, everybody is biting the apple. Negative breeds negative. Positive breeds positive. You get what you focus on. Focus on the right things, you will get the right things. That simple. Keep things simple. Don't be easily influenced. Realize that there is a lot of noise in the world, and because of that noise, most people are walking around truly accelerated, on-guard—reactive. All bad qualities for becoming a Champion. Live simply, like the old K.I.S.S. principle my mom would tell me about—keep it simple stupid. The old K.I.S.S. principle reigns true to date.

Here is the way I look at it, everything is usually based on just a few simple things. Take business for example. Find a hole in an industry that isn't being served properly. Create or find a product. Market the product better than anybody else by highlighting the benefits. Tell more people about it than your competition. Charge for your product. Innovate your product. Repeat. That is business 101. No complexity. Not complicated.

That process is very simple, linear, and easy to understand. The problems start when we start ask too many questions, like how? As the great Art Williams says, "How? You just do it. And you do it. And do it. And do it." *How?* is a dangerous question that can make you so analytical you forget what you have even set out to do!

You want to be a hitter in baseball. My high school coach once told me how to do it. "See it and hit it. That is hitting. Then, go hit more than everybody else and you will be better than everybody else. You will go further than everybody else. That is hitting. That is winning. That is how you get to the big leagues!"

Champions are simple people that keep things simple. They execute the daily fundamentals with consistency, habit, and focus. They do not deviate. They keep it very vanilla. No frills. Just results. Ever wonder how championship teams are built? The same way. On simplicity. On fundamentals. On respect. On simple standards that all agree upon.

They are built on understanding player strengths and weakness. Leadership of winning teams bring in complementary skill sets to make up for other player weaknesses. Each person on the team becomes a Champion because of the person next to them. That's teamwork. That's the essence of a winning formula.

Simple goals. Simple mission. Never getting too high or too low along the journey. That is how you become a Champion. Those are Champion-like habits.

THREE

Consistency Over Time Yields Results

"Consistency over time yields positive results." This is my favorite quote of all time. It is in my opinion the true differentiator between those who are Champions for life, on and off the field, and those who are just a flash in the pan. Consistency is a habit.

Consistency over the long haul is a true demonstration of discipline and positive focus. One of my best friends, longtime New York Yankees Equipment Manager, Rob Cucuzza, would always say, "He is hot right now, but let's see who he really is in the next three months."

Sure enough, we would always see that player fade. Usually around that ninety-day mark! We don't just call Robbie, Yoda, for the hell of it. His time on the job, his ability to analyze and understand player behaviors and tendencies, combined with his Bronx *gut instinct* leads to his brilliance when it comes to player and people assessments.

You see, anybody can get hot for a few months, but can they sustain it? How about that new employee or teammate who comes on board and has everybody in a panic because of their wicked results? An incredible first and second quarter. Then, they fade like a shooting star. Back to reality. Their reality.

You know what the greatest part about sports is? Stats. Stats tell you the story over the long haul. If a player is a career .220 hitter, the chances of him hitting .220 are far greater than him hitting .300. That is what makes the hiring process in business so tough. Applicants give personally selected and vetted references—they submit a resume they get to build and make-up. Neither of which of which are validated and based on actual results. Talk about a bias and unfair advantage in favor of the applicant. This is the root of all problems in the talent selection process. Speculation rather than absolutes. Storyline over stats. Highlight reel over reality.

The great Major League Pitcher, Mike Mussina used to always hold court and bless us with his famous words, "You are what you are." Brilliant. He is a Stanford grad, but his simple brilliance is much appreciated. Never be worried about somebody that is having short-term success. They can almost always be taken down by themselves. Their stats will tell you who they are. Believe them. Unsuccessful people are consistent too. Never forget that.

With Championship Habits, you have stick to your plan, especially if it was intuitively manufactured and well-thought-out when you created it. Stay the course. Keep your values front and center, and never go against your own word, gut, and integrity. If you can commit to that, day in and day out, you are already a Champion.

How many of you have ever started a workout plan or a diet? Have you stuck with it? Probably not. Why not? Well, Thanksgiving is next week. My wife's birthday is this weekend. I didn't pack a lunch. All the reasons why you failed. Excuses and lack of a true mission, commitment, goal, vision, and purpose towards a cause and outcome is why fail. Most people can commit for a day or week, but not for a lifetime.

This is why many believe success starts in the home. How we are raised influences who we become in many cases, but definitely not all. If you were allowed to put your shoes on the table and eat with your hat on, chances are, you will always leave your shoes on the table and eat with your hat on. That is the reality. You are who you are—unless you raise your standards and decide to change.

But consistency also works for positive outcomes as well. This is why whenever I speak to a team or company, I speak about the importance of habits and high standards. The standards part, I borrowed from Coach K of Duke. I love that word and the meaning he has brought to it.

What standards do you hold yourself to? What are the habits that make you who you are? Do you clean up after yourself when you spill milk as you are mixing your coffee at Starbucks? Or, do you wait for one of their employees to do it? When you knock something over in a store, or decide against buying something, do you pick the item up or leave it where it falls? That item that you decided against, does it end up back where you got it or does it just get placed wherever you are the time of the decision? All these little things matter. In my training facilities I would have sign that said, "Losers don't make their bed." Harsh. Aggressive. Not one hundred percent true, but a conversation starter about standards and the standards you hold yourself to.

Who are you? What do you stand for? I fight every day to stand for excellence. It is a commitment to self.

It can be exhausting. It can be frustrating at times. But it comes down to always doing what you say you are going to do and acting in accordance to that. How are you acting and behaving when nobody else is watching? This is the big test for college students entering their freshman year. No more mom and dad to wake you up, make your bed, and pack a bagged lunch. You are now fully responsible for you. (which you should have been once you were able to *think for yourself*)

In life, you have to get up and make the choice to win every single day. And, it *is* a choice. Do you help somebody in need or just walk past them like they are vagrant garbage? Do you help somebody that is having a bad day by being an ear to listen?

What do you stand for day in and day out? I don't care who you are today if you can't be that same person tomorrow. Nothing is scarier than somebody that is one person today and another person tomorrow. A

Jekyll and Hyde personality is hard to trust, predict, and engage with. So, if you come across one, run.

Coaching Tip: Consistency over time yields the greatest results.

Whenever I do media interviews, I am always asked, "What makes the great players great?" What makes the best CEO's the best?

Simple. High Standards. Great Habits. Consistent every day. These people don't necessarily out-work their competition, but they win over the long haul. Their percentage of consistent daily execution is off the charts. They chop at the tree every day until it falls. No matter how big the trunk, they take one swing at a time. Eventually, it falls. This is what Champions do. Consistency over time is what yields the result.

One of my favorite questions to ask successful people is, "How did you do it?" I have to laugh at their answer because it is always the same. "I am not really sure. It was a curved path. Definitely not linear. Ups and downs. But, I just worked hard every day and built something great. I showed up every day and remained consistent. I had no idea it would be this big."

Same story all the time. As a young business person, I had always looked for a step-by-step guide to building a business and would get pissed that I couldn't find it. Fifteen plus years later, I finally got my answer as to why I haven't found that book. It doesn't exist! There isn't a book on business that is legit.

Want to know why? Every person has a meandering path different from the next person. Your path is part of who you are—your experiences, your history, likes, dislikes, preferences, disposition, and demeanor. All of that determines your path.

I've always felt like success is actually a dumb word because it has so many meanings. So many definitions. But one thing I know for absolute sure about success is this is this—if you want to win in business, find something you love and go after it with everything you've got. Be consistent every single day. Never quit unless you run out of passion. Then you have to quit. But as long as that passion is there, swing the axe. Swing it hard. Swing to win. When the passion dies, get out immediately. Do not ask the questions, just get out and keep moving. Life will sort itself. You will learn the *why* later.

Never underestimate the power of hitting a single. As my good friend Barry once told me, "Singles every day lead to runs on the board. Singles are a symbol of consistency. Singles are the foundational building blocks of long-term growth and winning."

Consistency. Never forget that word. Be who you are today, tomorrow, and every day after that. Work today like you will work tomorrow. Be consistent. People love consistency. Consistency leads to trophies, rings, plaques, and championships.

While we are on the topic, you can't mention consistency and not mention the G.O.A.T., Mo Rivera. The greatest closer of all time. Game on the line, he is your guy. But what many do not know about the Sandman is that two innings before heading out to the bullpen, he was on his back, listening to salsa music, getting stretched and massaged by yours truly.

Every, single, game. When that 5th inning came around, if I didn't have his green tea and a granola bar waiting, he was not a happy man. Screaming my name like a lunatic throughout the clubhouse. He was consistent, and he expected consistency. That was his method.

Without a doubt, this was who he was. There was a right way and a wrong way. You better be doing things right—all the time. That was the expectation. That was his standard. If you agreed to something, you better deliver. I gotta tell you, he tested me. There were times, when I was in the bathroom at the start of the inning and boy did I hear it. "Where were you? Why were you not here?" Jokingly of course, but behind every great joke is the undertone of seriousness.

Religious and humble, Yes. But he would gut you faster than a fish he caught in his hometown of Puerto Caimito, Panama. Exceed expectations with your consistency. You will be rewarded for it.

When I take on new coaching clients, before we engage in any professional relationship, I always make them take an intake survey. I want to see how committed they really are to their goals. I want to see if they have a mission and purpose greater than themselves. How much pain do they have eating away at them, driving them towards change?

Why would I waste my time with somebody that isn't "all-in"? What's the point? That goes against my integrity and I'm setting myself up to fail. When people are experiencing *true pain* of any kind that is when they are most apt to make a radical change and stick to the process long-term. Also known as staying consistent. You want to work with me? Get seriously committed about being consistent.

The greatest coaches in the world are the ones that demand accountability, which is just becoming committed to yourself and what you say you're committed to. Your actions match your mouth. Get consistent. Make consistency your number one habit. That consistency will lead to winning.

Be consistent all the time.

FOUR

If They Don't Respect Your Time, They Don't Respect You

Words to live by. Spoken by the Yankees Captain, Derek Jeter once again. How many times have you had a meeting or appointment scheduled and somebody cancels at the last minute? You rearranged your entire day, shuffled your deck, and then it happens, the false apology: "I'm sorry, I can't make it. Something came up."

What blows my mind about this, is if that meeting would yield them a guaranteed return of $10,000, something tells me they would be there. Even if it was closer to $1,000, I'm sure they would be perky and on time.

Again, are you a person of your word? Do you value the time of other people? Or, do you see yourself as better than others and can manipulate people and time however you choose?

I remember when Jeet first said this to me. I was in Boston with the team. We had a four o'clock game that afternoon on FOX, and on those days many players loved to get their workout in early. Especially since we had to work out in the Red Sox weight room. Which, depending on what happened the night before, was either very relaxed or had tension so thick you could cut it with a knife.

One morning in particular, after getting to the hotel gym bright and early, I was supposed to meet one of our star players for a 10:00 a.m. workout. Time was ticking, and he was a no-show. I waited and waited. I gave up my personal workout, my breakfast, and my personal time. Sucked.

On a positive note, my next session was with Derek. Upon arrival, he warmly greeted me with, "What are you doing here so early, man?"

I explained that I had been waiting for another player who was a no-show. Then he said these words that would forever change my life.

Let me tell you something. If somebody does not respect your time, they do not respect you.

I couldn't agree more. The more time I spend thinking about it, the more I recognize that we honor the things that are most important to us. We honor the people we respect the most by being on time, ready to serve and faithful to our commitment to them. Just think, if you had a hot date waiting for you, you bet your backside we are on time.

Your favorite band playing live in concert. Once again, on-time. That business meeting you have been waiting a month to have—you know, the one that could have the huge contract attached to it? On-time. Lunch with somebody we do not care for? Cancel or late. Not all the time and not everybody, but the chances are definitely higher.

Whenever somebody says something so profound as Derek did that day, I always take an inventory of my own life and behavior. I have to admit, there have been instances that I did not honor my own commitments. That was a weakness for sure, but also a lack of respect for the other person's time. It gets me sick just thinking about it.

We're all guilty of actions we're not proud of. It is our job though to identify our negative, bad habits, self-correct, and change. If we can do that, we honor ourselves and our deficiencies. We all have them, so let's all be real with ourselves. Anybody who thinks they are perfect is definitely a tarnished stone.

Coaches Tip: The great lesson of sports I learned early on is the Vince Lombardi rule: If you are not 15 minutes early, you are late. This is more than about being on time. It is about respect.

I feel like every coach in my youth would mention it. To this day, I pride myself on always being on time. But we can all run late at times due to traffic or unexpected turbulence. If that is the case, call or text and let your "date" know. If you do this, you are covered and you're a pro not a schmo.

With Derek, we would work out and train Monday, Wednesday, and Friday at 3:00 p.m. every week. If he was running even a few minutes late, there was a call. Not just a call though, a call with a plan and an *audible*.

The audible was usually, "Let's get it in right after batting practice. I will be there right after I take my ground balls." With Derek, it was all about preparation and habit. It was all about respecting others. He had a running to-do list and checklist to greatness and Champion-like behavior. Working out was one of those items on his list. He and others like him are masters of their own schedule.

If you can master your schedule, the greater your chances for success and consistent results and behaviors will be. The lesson in this chapter is to honor your commitments. Honor your schedule. Hold yourself accountable. And, always remember to *respect* your own time, because the same holds true for you. If you do not respect your own time, you do not respect yourself.

Coaching Tip: Honor your commitments. You made them. Stick to them. You now must be a person of your word.

Time is our most limited resource. We all get the same amount. How do you use it? How do you deploy yourself to make sure you can maximize your impact and execution of things?

I am totally guilty. When I was younger (even 3 weeks ago), sometimes to save a buck, I would overextend myself. Even for silly things, like driving an hour to save twenty dollars. You have to drive an hour back too! So, own your time. Sometimes it's worth it to pay a few cents more per gallon for gas. Or, to take the toll road to save on the traffic. Some of those small choices over time can wear you down without you being aware of it. Stress. Fatigue. Take the short way home and pay the toll!

Coaching Tip: If you feel you are "stuck" or not going anywhere fast, start by owning your schedule.

Get yourself a paper planner and build your day based around your training and exercise. I am biased because I am a performance coach, but what is true is that if you take care of yourself first, you have taken care of your most important priority. You will then have more to *give*. You must *be selfish to be selfless.*

Similar to the speech by Admiral William H. McRaven, where he advises to "Make Your Bed," each morning, because if you do, you have accomplished your first task of the day. Taking care of yourself first is a winning formula.

We are all fulfilled when we accomplish something. The more you accomplish, the more fulfilled you will be if you base those accomplishments on the right factors and they're driven by the right mission. Progress. We all want to feel like we're progressing and moving forward. That leads to epic levels of personal satisfaction.

The human mind needs to remain active and centered. Another way of saying, "mission focused". The more focused you are towards your achievements, the better you will feel. As long as you align those achievements with your mission, vision, and goals. This is why your time is so critical. Use time to achieve greatness and win personal championships, rather than waste it on insignificant things, conversations, arguments, scrolling, surfing, and people that don't deserve it. I believe the greatest gift we can give ourselves is respect for our time and that of others.

Coaching Tip: Take out a sheet of paper and write *all* of your habits that are causing you to waste time. These could be social media scrolling, having too many open windows on your computer, not having a daily to-do list. Whatever it may be, write it down. Then, keep it in front of you.

Personally, I find that if I do not hit the ground running in the morning, setting my plan the night before, I feel like I am playing catch-up and guessing the entire next day. I lose my conviction, and my execution is almost always off. My production sucks and that causes a downward spiral in my mood and attitude. I am not progressing but falling behind on my own watch and expectations.

Coaching Tip: Get things done early. Plan for success. Take some of that time you typically blow to build a solid plan.

One thing I am also conscious of is what I call my associations. Everything we do in life has a cause-and-effect reflex. What does that mean?

An example for me is drinking coffee. I know. Silly, right? But when I drink coffee, I crave something sweet with it. If I am looking to spend my time getting into great shape, I should stop drinking coffee. Or, break the association reflex. That is a choice. If I plan my meals though, my foods and workouts provide me enough energy to not need the coffee. Then, the result is zero sweets and cravings.

What negative associations do you have? Another example of my own negative associations: When I have my social media windows open on my laptop, my production is down. Lack of focus. In and out of focus. Why? I prefer to see what others have going on than doing my work. That is the truth sometimes. So, what do I do? No tabs are allowed to be open except the one I am working on. Discipline. Another secret ingredient to the blueprint of champion performances. Fight your urges until they become tamed.

Rigid? Yes. Strict? Yes. But it is what has to get done for my behavior to be that of a Champion.

Coaching Tip: Write all of those associative distractions you have, and those behaviors that cause you to make other bad decisions.

The most important thing is being conscious of your issues. Awareness yields change if you will acknowledge those issues exist. Dig in, my friends. Take an inventory on yourself. Be honest. Respect yourself. Respect your time. Remember, if you don't respect your time, you don't respect yourself. If you don't respect the time of others, you don't respect them. Simple.

FIVE

Off Days Are Off Days

This chapter of the book goes out to all the Type-A overachievers out there. You know who you are. The folks who consider a vacation, sitting in a lounge chair in the Dominican Republic with a laptop (or tablet) on their knees, phone in one hand, a drink in the other, a Cohiba, and telling their significant other they are reading a kindle book while secretly making sure their work isn't piling up.

You know it's wrong. I don't have to tell you that. But, you can't stop. It is how you have been trained. It is the addiction. Leadership does it. Your co-workers do it. Your *work culture* is telling you do to it, and you are actually starting to believe it's okay.

Wake up. Those other people who are doing that sort of thing have the same problem as you. They are working with false progress. More is better. Not realizing the things that are eroding around them. Let it start with you. What is really happening? You are becoming institutionalized. Similar to that of Brooks from the movie, Shawshank Redemption. You can no longer live a normal life outside of work. Sad. Scary. Real. A true epidemic plaguing millions who have decided to give up their own life for the dreams of others, or the ones they *thought* they had as young ambitious whipper snappers.

Are you one of those people who is so badly wanting to get ahead, combined with a deep-down feeling of "not good enough?" You feel that no matter how much you do, how much you give, you feel as if it is not enough? Been there. I had to realize this was a personal problem, and I was using work to mask it. I was abusing myself creating to-do lists that never ended, scheduling meetings that did not matter, and complaining of how overworked and tired I was for the circus of nonsense I brought to town.

What does that lead to, besides high-guilt vacations? Never turning off. Like a radio that is plugged in for too long, frying out is the result if the cycle can not be broken. Eventual burn-out and performance decline are inevitable. Maybe even a nervous breakdown to top things off. You know, the kind where you stomach is so jacked up that you feel like you can vomit on command. A jaw so clenched your new nick name is Pitbull. Or, what about the chronic neck, back, and shoulder pain your can not seem to get rid of even with the best physical and massage therapy program around. But, since you are a problem-solver, a full prescription of Xanax in your bag at all times will do the trick. A ten-mg hit of oral bliss to take your body and mind from stress to rest. Makes sense.

As long as those little peace nuggets are ready to go should the time come for a mandatory deployment, it's all good.

Sad.

But again, you are not alone. Millions of people a year fall victim to mounting sick days and vacation days they never use because the company that issues them is the same company that shuns their use. This puts us in the panic attack era. Where more workers are going down for no real reason outside of over-work, overwhelm, and the inability to turn off their brain!

Question for ya. How many vacation, sick, and personal days do you have? Do you feel guilty using them?

Maybe you Coach a team and are afraid to give your players a day off because that is not the standard. Hustle. Grind. Work. The anthem of the modern day success seeker. Words of a poisoned brain that does not realize the value of rest and recharge and the positive effects on performance. Once again, guilty as written here. I used to feel that if I took a day off, I was letting somebody else down. I was not working hard enough to get to the top. I was showing my weakness and inability to keep going. I was basically soft. Trophy-generation type soft. A real "sissy" if you know what I mean.

I tell you what though, we can all learn something from a Professional Sports Schedule & Elite Athlete. Some may argue with me that the Professional Sports Season is too long and doesn't have enough off-days. But, where else can you find a job with such great perks and healthy lifestyle habits? You have to train for a living, eat well, and make sure your body and mind are in optimal shape at all times.

You read that correctly. How would this sound to you?

Work eight months out of the year. When you work, you get to travel and see the whole country three–four days at a time. They load your plane with water, drinks, great food, and snacks. On the days you have to "work," you can sleep in until 11:00 a.m. or noon. You have to be at work by 3:00 p.m., sometimes 4:00 p.m. Once you arrive, your clothes (which are washed for you from the day before and hung up in your personal locker), are ready to go. You change into them.

At that point, you head into the hot tub, soak for twenty minutes with your teammates. After that, you depart the tub, head in to see your Strength Coach for a personalized stretch and workout for about forty minutes, then grab a bite to eat and head out to the field to stretch again. Then, you hit and throw.

Sound good so far? I'm not done yet! After batting practice, you head in for a pre-game meal (which is great), then stretch again and head out for a two to four-hour game. Post-game, you hit the cold tub, shower, and grab a bite to eat from a first-class restaurant. After a long day, you hit the hay by midnight and do it all over again.

This is for eight months. Once the eight months are over, you have four months to rest and relax. The only expectation is that you train five days per week during the off-season and are ready to go come February 15th.

That, my friends, is the true definition of Balance and Recovery. Not some B.S. work, life balance speech you can find in your local Whole Foods holistic magazine that talks about ideal situations vs. the real world. Or, the walking off the bacon program that nobody uses in your Company.

What I failed to mention here is that there is a tremendous amount of expectation and performance anxiety that can take place during those eight months. This makes the rest and recovery that much more important. High expectations often lead to overworking, lack of balance, and stress. But, in sports, most of the players realize that if they do not recover, they can't sustain long term play.

In business, there is no thought of injury, so most go until they break. Not even considering fatigue leads to mental breakdown, a lack of focus, and sucking at your job.

Now I ask: How many high-level CEOs and executives run a schedule like that of professional athletes? Not many. The smart ones do though. They get it. What do I mean?

I already ran through the schedule of a pro athlete (baseball specifically). Now, let's talk about our typical CEO and executive in greater detail than we already have.

Gets up at 5:00 a.m. The smart ones grab a high or low intensity workout (based on how they feel) with a trainer to keep them accountable, planned, and focused for an hour. They shower, dress, skim the paper, and are soon out the door running to work. They may grab a bite to eat before they leave the house, but the great ones know they can supplement a good breakfast with a Venti Caffeine Bomb with Half and Half on the low energy days. Just kidding—kind of. That can most definitely carry you through lunch.

Arrival at the office! Aka Game-Time. Check the emails (which is usually continued from the car or train), look at their schedule, and boom, their meeting schedule begins. Meeting after meeting. In person followed by a conference call. This goes on for hours. Then it's lunch time.

Do I stay here at my desk and get more done? Or, do I head out to a lunch meeting where I will attack the breadbasket, have a social drink, and the lunch specials? Both choices are poor.

Lunch is done, then we have the afternoon calls and meetings. This goes on until about 5:30 p.m. At that point, there is a dinner meeting, event, or quick fly by to show face (even though none of the three are of any interest). All delaying the desire to just get back home, change into pajamas, and start the mental erosion process from the day.

Ah. Then we have rush-hour traffic as we head home. How could this be at 8pm? Starving, we look for a quick grab and go snack from a 7-11 or local WaWa (usually high carbs or sugar) to false-nourish us until we can get home. At that point, we are so tired and delirious, who has any desire to entertain the monotonous conversation of our significant other.

We listen inattentively, hoping to just turn on some sports or mindless television to get us to bedtime. We sleep for six hours, sometimes less after scrolling our phone for any last-minute fires that need to be handled. This is our life Monday through Friday.

Some weeks we are even lucky enough to travel to Asia or Europe, or the cross-country jam for a few days then head on back to our routine. Since we're flying halfway across the world or country for just a few days, might as well pack in as many meetings as possible, followed up by the justification, "I can sleep on the plane."

Brilliant. Years and years of this. Crammed in a Business Class seat (which is basically a coach seat of yesterday). Weight gain over time along with steady blood pressure elevation, psychological distress, and chronic back, neck, and shoulder pain has the entire business world now discussing "work life balance" and "mindfulness".

What a joke. But, more lives are lost to this routine than we can account for. Chasing success without rest. Whenever I work with CEOs and executives, either privately or through consulting with their company, I run them through this skit. I also share with them the formula that can lead to premature death.

STRESS + STRESS = STRESS

This usually stops them in their tracks. Have you ever heard of the story that involves a middle-aged CEO or executive, who is in great shape, runs five miles a day and lifts weights, and has also completed many marathons or triathlons? Then, suddenly, one day he or she is out training and has a massive heart attack?

"Can you believe so-and-so just had a heart attack and dropped dead? They were in such great shape! You see? That's why I don't exercise that much." *Wink.*

This is classic for the Type-A leader or success chaser. This person cannot function without a full deck and schedule in front of them. They need to always have something to do. Resting is not an option outside of "vacations."

Why does this happen? Stress from work. Stress from working out (which many don't realize is deadly with a taxed and maxed stress level already on their body). I get so frustrated with many magazines that publicize exercise as being the best recipe to reduce stress. That is a lie unless you preface what type of exercise. High intensity exercise, boot camps, and high mileage endurance is not a good combination with a highly stressed person. The body can only take so much, and it will interpret this higher intensity exercise as more stress. That combo is that knockout punch.

So, when you are feeling stressed, the preferred exercise is to walk, hike low altitude, stretch, bike, get a massage and stretch, or hit the sauna, but stay away from high intensity. Your focus during this period is not to get a six pack, but rather get your health back. Rebalance your body. Get your stressed organs to *chillax*. Now that we've cleared that up, let's get back to Off Days are Off Days.

The best athletes in the world get this. If you do not rest after heavy bouts of work and training, you will break. What can you as a business person or leader do to conquer this issue? Simple.

Rebuild your work day putting yourself first. Schedule the rest and relaxation. Schedule the times to grind it out and work. You need to understand that your physical and mental state is what it is for a reason. You do not just wake up shot. It results from your daily choices, routines, schedules, and habits. If you want more out of your body, give it more rest, not more work. That is not lazy. It is smart.

So, let's talk about it.

Example: In bed by 10:00 p.m., sleep at least six to seven and a half hours. Get up, hydrate, stretch, and get your workout in. How you feel determines your training. If you feel great, get after it. If you feel tired, sluggish, and dragging, start slow and modify. Finish your training and grab a shower. Give yourself positive self-talk while washing your pits. Post shower, sit down, have a nice breakfast with some healthy choices, a cup of tea or coffee, and read the paper or talk with your family. Then, after you feel settled, head out to work.

Listen to some music (or a positive podcast) in the car, appreciate the elements, and plan your day in your head covering all of your objectives you want to accomplish. Arrive. Three short meetings and a few calls in the morning, break them down with follow-up steps and needs before lunch. Get up and socialize with your team, then head to lunch. Solo with a book or take one of your young staff members with you to help with their development. Then, after lunch, three more short meetings, a few phone calls, then pack up.

If you have an event or dinner at night, before heading there, wrap up your day early enough so that you can go for a walk, maybe round two at the gym, or grab a short twenty to thirty-minute massage and head out for your nightcap. Remember, you call the shots in your life. Don't drag the meeting out if you don't have to—unless you are having a blast and have a light morning scheduled the next day with a late start. Since you own your schedule, you should have already planned this.

Once you get home, take some time to unwind before heading to bed. Wash your face, brush your chops, floss, rinse, and hit the sack. That my friends, is a much better day. Will they all go that smoothly? Maybe. But a rule of thumb I abide by, is only working in thirty, sixty, or ninety-minute blocks. Never more.

Never forget to play offense on your own life. Take ownership of it. The good, the great, the bad, and ugly. You are the proud, or not so proud owner.

Also, I am goal focused. Once I achieve my objectives for the day, I am done. No matter what! Finish, then take time for you to relax.

Now, let's also talk about looking at your year in seasons. We all know that business has seasons. The slowest seasons of the year are December through January 1st. The month of August (July is slow too), and the week of Thanksgiving.

I am amazed at how many people are still surprised when these weeks come just how dead it is. Hello! It is like that only every single year.

Since we have this data, you should look at this as your off-season. A great time to plan your vacations, have later arrivals and earlier departures. Just a solid time to put some of your personal goals up front. This is not a ticket to be lazy, but when it is work time, much like the athletes during game time, you get after it with a ferocious tenacity to win. That is Champion behavior.

Champion behavior is not working until you drop. Champion behavior is not crushing your staff until they break. Be smart. Push, but don't over-push. If you can take this in, make the adjustments, you can win big. Bigger than ever.

As a Leader, you should also be smart and aware enough to recognize when your staff is smoked. If you see this, rather than waiting for them to ask for a half day, or a full day off, you take initiative and give it to them. This will go a long way in the respect and "Great Boss" categories. It is not about you walking around and beefing up your team's ego. It's about understanding them and their needs as individuals. We are all unique and must be treated as such. Recognize it!

Personally, I learned this the hard way. Growing up as an athlete with high expectations for myself, my mentality was always, "If I am not working and training, somebody else is." This is all crap. These are B.S. lessons low level coaches feed into the DNA and minds of their players. It could not be further from the truth. Or, what leadership guru's are selling at conferences to bait HR professionals hook, line, and sinker. There are no secrets. Just common sense. Which, is becoming an extinct resource with higher levels of enablement and coddling.

I still can not process how lame this advice is. This, for me, created a really dangerous mentality because I trained to train. No goals and objectives outside of more training equals better performances. Work all the time. Work every free minute you have. This way, nobody can call you lazy and nobody is out-working you. My focus was on not being outworked. Not on winning at my mission, vision, and goals. I was time-focused and not results-focused. And, I was focused on others more than myself, in a bad way. I did not see Secretariat looking back to see how far the other horses were behind him. Good lesson for life.

The best players I have ever been around, Hall of Fame types, worked less than everybody. They knew what *they* needed and did nothing more. They covered all of their objectives. Taking care of their body and mind was their #1 priority. They knew exactly how much they needed to practice and how much they could practice without it negatively affecting their ability to play the game.

Corporate culture today in most places is a joke. Everybody is acting busy, scrolling their smartphone, and checking emails like savages. Most are going nowhere. I would bet that actual total work that gets done on average by people during a day's work is actually only three to four hours. Now, if you head to work from 9:00 a.m. to 5:00 p.m., over 50 percent of your time is not even productive.

And, on the other end, most companies have all these Huffington Post conjured up "initiatives" that are there just to say, "we did it," in most cases, rather than providing actual value that we can measure past the bottom line, but more on the metric of a thriving, happy, producing workforce.

In my opinion (which can be snarky), we do not have a work-life balance problem here in America. We have a poor scheduling, culture, and expectation problem. Just a thought, but what if companies told their staff to come in for four hours and for the remaining four or five hours of the day, you can work from home? Just be available, but you can work from anywhere. Or, come in and work for three or four hours and if you have a meeting in the afternoon, come back for that. Or, if you are a morning person, you work on flex schedule that accommodates your natural clock. If you are a night person, your flex schedule gets you to work by noon and out by eight o'clock.

Crazy thoughts, right? Not so much. Just wait until more millennials hit the workforce. Things are changing and will continue to change. If you do not make these changes as corporate leaders, you will find your employees more focused on their side-hustle than on their primary-hustle.

The focus needs to always be on productivity and vitality, not on time.

Time is not a true measure of accomplishment. I know people that have been working for forty years and have accomplished nothing. Look at people like Mark Zuckerberg. He accomplished more by the end of his college career than some in a lifetime.

When you think scheduling, efficiency, and productivity, you win. And you have a life. A life that can be balanced on its own, without a formal meditation program, if you follow these rules.

Now, I want to be perfectly clear here. I am not saying let the inmates run the asylum or create a work culture that is as soft as butter. I do not stand for that. But, take a look at the operation you have running and see what changes you can make to get your engine running tighter while getting the most out of your people.

Smart people are efficient people. Smart people accomplish more per hour than others. I would bet they are also more rested with more movies, episodes of Billions under their belt, and recreational activities than their overworked counterparts. You know the ones. The ones who arrive early, stay late, don't get promoted, and make the same amount of money year after year (and can't stop bitching about it). Why not me? How did I not get that position? Same thing as the player that can't hit, is not in the line-up, and hates the coach for it. Makes sense, right? Ha.

We call that going nowhere. So, if you want to play the game for a long time and feel great doing it, prepare for that. Train for the long game. Own your schedule without it owning you. Always remember, Off Days are Off Days. Take them. That is why they give them to you. To take a few extra for yourself. Every day is game day.

SIX

3 Things...

One of the greatest players I have ever had the chance to work with was so much more than a great baseball player. This guy was a true modern-day philosopher, hyper-focused on simplifying the human thought process and emotional response—a magician of simplification. In a world that presents us with a tremendous amount of daily noise through marketing messages, sounds, sites, dings, bells, reminders, and alerts, concentration and focus can be hard commodities to come by.

I'm sure you can all relate. You sit down to do one thing and before you know it, five windows are open on your laptop, you are texting, listening to music, and finding the right channel to watch while you "work." In a world that once had only one screen, the TV, we can now manage up to three screens at once;

absorbing nothing—unfocused, jittery, and unable to home in on a target.

Crazy right? And once again we wonder why we can't get things done. With that, let me introduce you to one of the greatest philosophies I have ever encountered on the subject of getting it done by none other than the great Number 42, the GOAT, Mariano Rivera.

A man that grew up with nothing more than a fishing pole, a soccer ball, and a baseball glove made of a milk carton, he has abundant wisdom on keeping life very simple and slow. Ice in the veins. Extreme clarity between the ears. Minimal to no voices.

It was a cold January day in Harrison, New York when Mo called me over to his house for a mid-day workout and stretch. After doing some lifting, we set up the massage table, and I took him through a stretch and massage session. During the season, deep conversation is possible, but it often gets interrupted by other players or major distractions like men on base or a dwindling lead late in the game.

On this day I had to ask him a question that had been burning me up since I was about fourteen years old watching his debut at Yankee Stadium in 1995.

Very simply, I put his leg down mid-stretch and said, "Mo, how do you do it?"

"Do what buddy?"

"How do you get it done night after night? The biggest situations, game on the line, and the crowd going wild. How do you do it?"

As somebody who, as a kid, struggled with levels of performance anxiety and self-image issues, I had to know. How many people have the chance to ask The

Sandman such a deep question in the comfort of his home? I had to take advantage of this moment.

He finally responded after a light giggle. "Buddy, I do three things. First, I quiet the noise. Second, I slow everything down. Third, I throw one pitch a time."

My instinctive response was, "That's it? But what else do you do?"

"That's it, buddy. That is all I do. The most important thing you can do is quiet the noise."

Now, do you think I would let him off the hook with that answer? No way.

I went on to ask, "But what about the big situations? The World Series. Game seven. The biggest of the big."

Then he hit me with the magic. "Buddy, in life, there are no *big* situations. Big situations do not exist. No situation is bigger than another unless we make it bigger. We have the choice. But every situation is the same. We decide. We make situations big. They are all the same."

That was amazing and a defining statement for me. It changed my life. Again, as a kid, I struggled with making situations bigger than they really were. They began to own me and my decision making. Eventually they affected how I viewed myself. Can you relate? It is amazing how the demons can get in our heads as young people and shape our thoughts through the future. Those simple thoughts of I am fat, I am ugly, I am not as good as so and so, and all the other mental savatage that comes so easily to the developing soul. Luckily, I had a very positive mother who told me three things: *don't take any sh%t from anybody* and *forget them, do your own thing* when I would come home with some boy drama. Tremendous advice for a young guy trying to find his place between the sports world and the drama / music department.

What Mariano taught me that day though, was priceless. Re-framing how I see the world and the situations that come across my path, is all under my control by changing how I view it. This is in line with the idea that what we think about, we give life to. Now, whenever a crap storm starts flying through my head, I remind myself to stay above it. If you sink your emotional state to the level of the problem, it gets bigger and steals your energy. I refuse to let that happen. One of the many things I would tell my younger self. Stay above the storm and in times of turbulence, elevate your thought process and go for gold.

Coaches Tip: What we think about, we give life to. What we think about, we can also give power to. Own your thoughts. They can be very rewarding or very dangerous. Get on a higher frequency and think above your problems and negativity. Protect your mind with positive visions of success.

Imagine the power of that. Nothing can rattle you if you don't let it. We have the choice. I feel like in today's world, society teaches us to obey and be subservient, but the common thread among successful athletes and entrepreneurs is that they just don't give a f * * *.

These athletes see things from their own unique perspective. They are the CEO and GM of their thoughts and actions. Often, this classifies them as egomaniacs or narcissists, but the reality is, they focus on what they want to focus on and what they see as important. That obsessive visualization and thought-ownership guarantees their achievements and successes.

The best-of-the-best typically have no idols and do not believe in or conform to social norms. They ignore the noise and focus on the things they can control. We have seen this written in personal development and psychology books for years. Yet, many of us are still victims in our own stories when we should be the superheroes.

My grandfather used to live by the serenity prayer. He was the most relaxed guy I ever met.

Coaching Tip: The Serenity Prayer: God, grant me the **serenity** to accept the things I cannot change; courage to change the things I can; and wisdom to know the difference.

Living one day at a time, enjoying one moment at a time, accepting hardship as a pathway to peace, taking, as Jesus did, this sinful world as it is, not as I would have it, trusting that He will make all things right, If I surrender to His will, so that I may be reasonably happy in this life, and supremely happy with Him forever in the next. Amen.

I will never forget the words of the great Number 42. Today, when something shakes me up, I take a step back and tell myself, "Don't give it energy. Don't give it power over you. Own your thoughts. Then, and only then will you own your results."

Another performance hack I deploy when worked up over something, is I activate myself physically..

Another way of saying I get my workout in followed by some sort of extreme temperature change like cryotherapy, steam room or sauna, and conclude with a cold shower. This blast of heart rate and temperature change allows me to stop focusing on the crap and get focused on building myself.

Something interesting happens to the body when you activate your physiology through work and temperature. You forget about what was bugging you. It's like switching the train track of your thoughts. Before you know it, you're headed to Santa Fe rather than Gotham City.

How often does something get you worked up and before you know it your mind is racing? Concentration and focus are gone. Effectiveness and productivity have gone with it.

First, you have to recognize it's happening. Take a deep breath. I also have a little thing I do while in the moment. It involves tapping my thigh with my hand multiple times, sometimes even giving myself a pinch or pulling the rubber bracelet I keep on my left wrist that says, *Compete with Confidence.*

Why? It takes my negative thoughts away and changes my focus towards my physiology rather than the self-created "issue."

Quiet the noise. Slow everything down.

One pitch at a time.

Could you imagine Mariano trying to be great if he had the TV on, phone on, laptop dinging, email going? Ok, now go pitch. Impossible. Obviously he would never have his phone on the field, but the dings and bells can be symbolic of errant thoughts, doubt, fear, self defeating words. Also known as *the noise.*

When you meet the grace of Mariano, it is almost like he is on the same fishing boat he grew up on as a kid, but all the time. Nothing gets him nuts. Well except laziness, excuses, and games that go entirely too long.

He handles everything with grace and poise. I would always say he was the equivalent of watching human poetry. If poetry could be a person, it would be him. Or, better yet, a still, motionless lake. His movements were deliberate and precise. Simple. No wasted energy. No wasted steps.

Where do you waste time and energy? What are the thoughts that own you? What are the patterns that dominate your mind? Who are the people who cause you angst? Identification of these things is critical to your short and long-term success. If you are determined to become a Champion, your behaviors must change. It all starts with identifying the problematic thinking and behaviors. Redirecting negatives is one of the most important *champion habits.*

We all have them. The sooner we can identify and self-correct, the sooner we are free to go out and win. It is easy to see who is struggling in a workplace. Study their body language, speech patterns, and the things they talk about and compare those to their productivity.

Negative thoughts and negative body language often equals lower production. What if that person could put the Mo Rules into play? They would realize what is actually bothering them and make a change. Chances are, they are giving a negative situation too much life and energy. That's killing them and their performance. Destroying their chances for internal peace and success.

Since this is becoming the chapter of Mariano, I will share a word he lives by. Passion. You must have passion in all you do. Passion drives results.

Coaches Tip: Passion Drives Results. Then, results drive more passion. The power of momentum is critical in both sports and business. As a Champion Leader, it is your job to create the momentum through mini-victories. A roaring blaze can begin by igniting even a morsel of your passion.

If something great motivates you like a clear mission and vision, putting passion to it is the secret ingredient to creating the kinetic fire. The key is combining that passion with a relentless subconscious belief that the divine universe is aligned with you. If your mission and vision are aligned with who you are and what you are meant to do, passion is already there and is along for the ride just waiting for a spark. Passion is the driver of the ride towards winning championships in life, sports, and business.

Any championship team will tell you they felt like they were being pushed and pulled at the same time towards the end goal of winning the whole damn thing. This is because everybody was working towards the same mission, vision, and goal. It was a communal goal that every person bought into. The players had immense passion for the process and no *outside* situation or conflict would get in the way of that mission and vision.

Have you felt this in any part of your life? Maybe when you got your first job and you kept advancing? Or, perhaps when you were in a relationship that just kept getting better and better? When you have that feeling, it is the *zone* that everybody references. Everything down to your core is in alignment. An amazing feeling.

We can create that feeling based on our decisions and the things we think about, the people we surround ourselves with, or the music we listen to. What we watch on television. The books, newspapers, and magazines we read. And, finally, by the amount of free, unplugged, quiet time we give ourselves to self-explore.

Take time every day to ask yourself if you took the time to quiet the noise, slow everything down, and throw one pitch at a time. Then ask yourself what you are giving too much life and energy to that is taking away from your happiness.

All the answers to life's questions will present themselves if you take the time to listen and feel. Take the time. Always remember The 3 Things.

SEVEN

Fit to Win.

Are your Fit to Win?

What do you mean Coach? If you mean do I look like a professional athlete, then no. Do I have to look like one in order to Win?

Nope.

Fit to Win doesn't mean you have to look like a professional athlete with forty-yard sprint times and vertical jump heights that are among the world's best. What it means is being fit enough, both physically and mentally, to play the game you choose to play. Sports. Business. Life.

Your preparedness to play will lead to undaunting confidence. Which, as well know, along with ability, is the true foundation of winning and success. Confidence. Gotta have it. It is not optional, but essential. Sports. Business. Life. They all take some level of training and fitness to endure and stay on top. Take parenthood as an example. If you are not in optimal health, how else can you be all you need to be for your children without falling into a deep health rut from lack of sleep or high stress at work?

What has always frustrated me is that we all want massive results in all areas of our existence, but we fail to realize that our foundation of health is everything. If you are not in optimal physical and mental condition, you can't win. You may want to win. But, you will never be a long term winner if you are falling apart and a human house of cards. You must be ready to play.

You may win short term with slob-like habits, with some quick get-rich opportunities, but in the end, you will realize those were just some luck-based successes built on quick yielding, decaying energy reserves. True success is about being able to win the long game. We have all seen that athlete or corporate Rockstar that is the talk of the town for three months and then fizzles like a firecracker, ending up broken in a backyard somewhere. They blasted off, peaked, then hit the ground. Most likely crashing into the ground. Hard. Very common.

Every team in professional sports has a position on their staff dedicated to the physical and mental welfare of their players. The correlation between optimal on-field play and training is extremely clear. A better conditioned player equals a healthier, higher performing player which leads to a healthier, higher performing team. It also helps the organization validate the size and length of a contract. An insurance policy, sort of.

How do I know? I held that position for many years with the New York Yankees Organization. My exclusive job responsibility was to keep players feeling good, pain-free, and ready to play at all times. Improving their speed, strength, power, nutrition, sleep habits, and recovery was my game. I was their performance coach and I loved the responsibility. They called me "Coach." Well, and a few other words when I asked them to do things they did not want to do.

I refer to my position as an asset manager of over three hundred million dollars in human capital. Protecting the Steinbrenner investment was what I was hired to do.

It was always a love, hate relationship between the players and me. I was the one that had to push them when they didn't want to be pushed, or, make them work at uncomfortable levels to help them cut weight or for their rehabilitation program. But, they knew they had to do it and they wouldn't have done it without the coaching. The power of coaching is amazing. So, if you do not have one, get one (hint, hint).

It has always blown my mind how companies that are seeking optimal results from their CEO, C-Suite, executives, and the entire team, invest minimal money to make sure their teammates are ready to play the most competitive sport of all; business.

Wall Street, shareholders, and leadership demand quarter over quarter victories but fail to look at the core fundamentals of how their company *works*, often ignoring the welfare of their *players* in a quest to keep expenses down. But, that investment into their *team* can yield tremendous dividends in less work days missed, higher productivity, and a vivacious energy than can drive the workplace culture and results to another stratosphere.

Many companies today have a ferocious turn-and-burn culture with extremely high churn rates, losing some incredible people, often because the company culture and demands are far greater than somebody is willing and able to meet or exceed long-term. Some of these individuals leave the corporate world and go on their own, where they can live a healthy lifestyle, accomplishing some remarkable feats in solo-preneurship.

I bring this up because companies are always discussing retention, productivity, and profits, but they are failing to realize how their company cultures and demands require people to be in world-class shape, without anybody qualified enough on the team to get them there. Which, when working fifteen-hour days is hard to achieve. The body will eventually break mentally or physically causing the teammate to quit or fail.

Why would a company not invest in keeping a coach on-staff to optimize executive and employee welfare? The importance of this was discovered in sports years ago, but never made its way to the corporate world. Sad, because some companies and leaders have the audacity to compare their organizations to that of a sports team, but they lack all the fundamental building blocks and ingredients that make up a sports team, mainly support for those *playing the game*. I get that many companies try by offering insurance savings or a health and wellness program, or, an afternoon walking club. But, many of these programs are doomed to fail before they start because they never get to know the true, individual needs of executives and employees. They roll out some standard app integrated wellness compliance program with minimal human interaction outside of an annual Cycle for Survival Event or Tough Mudder while they spend the rest of the year having employees track their steps, reading elementary school bulletin boards on health, and hosting team-building events that jaded employees want nothing to do with.

That equals Fail, not Win. That is not a championship plan. Whether you are an executive, employee, coach, or athlete, you must remember your health and fitness will determine your elevation and overall success. Teams that have an extreme level of preparedness mentally and physically win championships.

How do you handle failure? How do you handle stress? How can you handle working the late shift? How can you handle not getting a hit in days or hitting a free throw in weeks? How do you handle failure? Can you fail and not foreclose on yourself? These are all teachable skills that need to be trained.

Being Fit to Win comes from an early philosophy I had when training elite athletes, Out-Train Your Sport. Get yourself so fit mentally and physically that the challenges of the *sport* can't meet the rigors of your training.

Look at it like this: If you run five miles a day, but the test will only be for two miles, you have out-trained your sport.

Now, that is a very simple example relating to your endurance, but if we were relating this to failure, the best might say, "dream big, test small, fail quickly (and often). This way you get very comfortable failing. It won't scare you since you have already done it. As much as you have to be Fit to Win, you must also *fail to win*.

Failing by taking risks means you will put yourself out there. This is where growth happens. But if you will fail, you must learn how to do it. Chastising yourself is not the way. Re-framing your mindset is everything. Becoming Fit to Win for me has always been based on my concept of re-framing.

Coaching Tip: When something negative happens, or you fail, switch your thought process. Don't look at the failure, look at the win in the failure. No failing, only learning.

When something negative happens, or you fail, switch your thought process.

Example: You start a business, run it for five years, then run out of money to operate because sales are down. Do you stress, binge eat, stay up all night trying to figure it out, or do you concede after taking too much action to rectify the situation and it isn't working? You have to close, but that doesn't mean you failed. The business failed. You won because you took the risks and got in the game. You are ahead of 90 percent of the people who never tried. Now, dust off, get up, and get back at it.

The re-frame is about saying, "I didn't fail, the business did. Although I didn't take this business to the level I wanted, I learned tremendous skills and lessons I can apply to my next job or business. I won't make the same mistakes twice." That is a proper re-frame.

Re-frames help to reduce stress and the personal imprisonment many feel as the result of a venture-gone-wrong. Re-framing works for business, sports, relationships, or any other performance-gone-wrong. As my buddy Marc Roberge, from the band, Of a Revolution (OAR) says, "You gotta be wrong sometimes. Sometimes you are wrong, sometimes you are right. Just keep moving forward. That is what life is about. Speak to any high performer in business or sports. They will all recount many moments of failure before the big victory.

Being Fit to Win is about preparing for failure as much as success. Both require tools and skills to sustain for the short and long term. When I coach and consult with companies and CEOs, the first questions I ask are about their overall health and fitness levels. I work to learn as much as possible about their habits. Do they exercise every day? Do they eat well? Do they pack lunches and snacks? How many nights a week are they home for dinner? What do they say to themselves when they speak to themselves?

Many think these questions are nuts since they brought you in to better their business and you are speaking about their personal health and habits. On the surface it makes little sense. But if you can get the leadership healthier, this can often change the entire company culture to one of being Fit to Win.

An example of this is my client Brandon Steiner. Brandon is the founder and CEO of Steiner Sports, the top collectibles and memorabilia company in the world. Years ago, Brandon and I worked together to optimize his health and performance, so he can be a better overall performer and leader as he was heading into his fifties. The goal was to reduce his body fat, increase lean muscle, recalibrate is diet and nutrition habits. As we went through this process, he took all of the knowledge he had gained and brought it to his company.

Health and fitness became a priority for his company. If you wanted to work there, no fast food or pizza for lunch. He understood the relationship between being Fit to Win, not only for himself, but for his team and overall corporate success. His culture also started to let his employees know, hey, at Steiner we care about you not just as employees, but as healthy people. He got it. That is what it is all about. Winning.

We are all here to win bigger in life, work, and sport both for ourselves and the people/ organizations we serve. Habits will get you there. You base your habits on what you decide to focus on. The focus on increased revenue and profits, if gone about the traditional way of "grind it out," and "whatever it takes," will lead you to short-term gains, but eventually you will derail your train at some point. You will exhaust all your conductors and track personnel. !

Don't wait for a health scare or consistent poor performance to make a change. Investing in your health, fitness, and mental training can not only save your life, it can get you to your goals faster than you thought. The difference is, you are doing this in a healthy way. It may not be cool or sexy when judged by others, but who cares. We don't care what people think. We are on our own road to success. Fit to Win is based on the premise of being "selfish to be selfless".

My buddy, Ralphy, once said this to me. Amazing advice.

Coaching Tip: If you are in better condition, you can give more to others. Get yourself right, then give like a man-imal! (part man or woman and animal AKA #beastmode)

If you are in better condition, you can give more to others. You can be a better boss, parent, teammate, and overall performer. That is what Fit to Win is about. Physical strength, thriving lifestyle, and mental fortitude to endure any type of hell that may come your way.

That is how Champions become Champions. Are you and your company or team Fit to Win?

EIGHT

Torre Rules; People First.

When you have the opportunity in life to coach under a sports Icon like Joe Torre, there is a lot you can learn. When I first began working under "The Godfather," I was a nineteen-year-old kid with a dream and unwavering work ethic, open to learning and like a sponge when this man walked into the room.

We called him The Godfather, but he really was. With old school traditional values, a grandfather-like charm, and a style and grace that would make even Don Vito himself take a second look; this man was amazing. The biggest takeaway for me from the Torre era was simple; when you put people first, you win. The backbone of winning a championship is the group of Champions that go out to win every day. Whether it be a sports team, a household, or a work-force, the people are everything.

My good friend, Rob Cucuzza, would always say, "When there are more people in the cart than there are pulling it, you lose. When you have more people pulling the cart than sitting in it, you win. It's that simple." Peel this back. What does "sitting in the cart" mean? It means having people on your team willing to sit back and coast while others grind to move the entity forward. You can not win with these types of people. So, if they are on your team, time to send them out to pasture.

If you are a father who lets your wife do all the parenting and house work, you are in the cart.

If you are an athlete who cares more about personal stats and Instagram followers than team victories, you are in the cart. If you are a CEO or executive who only cares about fluffing your own numbers, even if you know in time the organization will come crumbling down, you are in the cart. If you are on a team of any kind allowing yourself to sit back while others pull the cart uphill, you are in the cart. Not only are you in the cart, you are the weakest link everyone talks about.

Being in the cart is symbolic of a loser mentality. When called out, those in the cart never think they are. If you ask them, they are pulling harder than anybody. I call those, excuses. Winners are 100 percent accountable to themselves, their team, and their organization at all times.

We all know who the winners are and those who are the overachievers. It's obvious. To the same extent, we all know who the dogs are. If you want to win, let the dogs out. As leaders, it is our job to quickly identify them, reward the winners, and release the losers.

The great Yankees General Manager, Brian Cashman, refers to these types people as "dead wood". They are just hanging around, eating up resources, but not producing. My long-time friend and co-worker, Steve Donohue, called them, "high maintenance, low output individuals."

You see, in sports, the faster you can identify, the faster you can release. I'm amazed to this day, how many CEOs I speak with, allow subpar attitudes and behaviors, and permit people on their teams only because their organization is *currently* winning. I emphasize the word *currently* because it is important to understand, just because you are winning today, doesn't mean you will be winning tomorrow. I love how Barbara Corcoran of Shark Tank approached her real estate business. Every year, she would cut the bottom ten percent of her workforce. Her lowest performers were sent out. Fired. Eliminated. How many of you lead a team or organization where you know somebody that is not pulling their weight but you allow them to stay on the team because your current numbers are good? Or, because you are too lazy to fire them? You pacify taking action by telling yourself "finding new talent is not easy" or "if we let them go, then we have to train new people and they may even be worse." Well, if that is your approach, you are not leading from a champions perspective. You are engaging in the same behaviors you are saying you do not want on your team. Get out of your own way. Ruffle some feathers. Take action and change your game to one of winning. Once you do, you will set a new tone with a very clear message: *we do not accept mediocrity here.* It always starts with top. This is why leaders need the most energy of all. They need the energy to make great decisions and to deal with the consequences.

I think it's time to realize that over time, this person (the dead wood) will cause distress among the others. People on teams are not stupid. They can quickly see when others are not pulling their weight. It gets frustrating over time. Unfortunately, most people on teams won't speak up to their supervisor. This leads to passive-aggressive behaviors and eventually an erosion of a great culture and, losing great talent. It becomes costly. Great talent will leave way before the junkyard dogs.

Like sports, if you lead an organization, don't be afraid to sign somebody's release papers if they are no longer performing. Once again, *no longer* is the emphasis. Just because somebody was once an asset and a high performer doesn't mean similar results are guaranteed in the future.

This is the biggest issue with long-term contracts in sports. You are paying on what somebody will do in the future, but you are determining their future value based on their past. That can be dangerous. People change. Lives change. Life changes people. There are many factors that go into a great performance over the long haul, but if you see somebody who used to be great, no longer being great, after a conversation with them about it, you may have to show them the door.

This is where the Torre Rules come into play. If you put your people first, you will know where your team is at all times. The same is true for yourself. Take an inventory of yourself to know where you are at all times. It is crucial for strong self-analysis and team analysis to keep things moving along in a healthy way.

Coaches Tip: Take an inventory of yourself to know where you are at all times. Personal introspection will take you places you could only dream of. Be honest with yourself. Are you as good as you think you are? Getting real with yourself is the first step toward victory.

Put people first. Life is not just about spreadsheets and stats. There is a place for them, but as soon as you forget that those who are responsible for those stats are human, you will be making decisions based on a false reality.

Stats are not an end to themselves. Get to know the people. Everybody needs an individualized approach to learning and management. If we treat everybody the same, we will make an epic mistake.

What made Hollywood Joe so good was that he never aired somebody out publicly. It was always in *confidence* behind a closed door. He handled it professionally with the best interest of the person at the forefront of the discussion. Everybody mattered. Their life mattered, even more so than who they were as a player. He wanted to know who they were as a person.

You can learn a lot about a person when you take a few minutes to ask, "How are you doing?" Especially when you mean it and actually care about their answer. How many casual "How are you doing" conversations do you hear in a day? (more if you are from the New Yawk area). How many of those asking care about your response?

This is a powerful question. Don't take the answers lightly. Listen. When you listen to another person, you will get all your answers. You will find your "why" and their "why".

I believe the biggest failure among most of the workforce is a lack of respect for each other. People in the workplace coexist, but do not truly have each other's back. This is what I love about the military. You must care for your brother. If not, you may lose your life because of it.

What if we approached our family and our work family the same way? Now, the thing to remember about respect is that it is earned, not just given. The more you give, the more you get when your character, integrity, and values remain strong. If you can be bought or sold, expect minimal respect.

And some words of wisdom from none other than Derek Jeter. "Everybody talks about respect. I believe that everybody should be treated fairly, but not everybody should be treated the same."

It's true. Should you treat a rookie like a veteran? I don't think so. Status is earned. That is a great thing. That is a motivating factor when somebody can see that their situation can improve over time, within the same organization, with a high level of performance over time.

In sports, should we treat seniors and freshmen on the team the same? Earn your stripes. That is how the world works. If you are a true All-Star and a great performer, you will move through the ranks faster than others.

Even though there are certain norms that exist, the better you perform, the more freedom you earn. The more respect you earn. Instead of looking at this as bad because we are all *equal*, just look at your own life. Did your parents treat you the same as a teenager as they did when you were a toddler? Of course not. You grew up, earned trust, earned respect, and in turn, more freedom as a result.

You determine your results. Therefore, you determine your freedom. In today's *freedom* culture, everybody wants CEO liberties while still holding an entry-level position collecting an entry level wage. It just don't work that way! Wouldn't we all want that? Entry level responsibilities with CEO pay. That though, would kill the American dream.

Coaching Tip: Let's commit to focusing less on our entitlements and more on what we earn through performance. Let's focus on bringing as much value as possible, rather than expecting to be paid a premium for bringing little to no value.

Elevate your performance and as a result, you will elevate in all other facets of life. As the late, great Jim Rohn would say, "If you want more money, bring more value." You are paid based on the value you bring to a team or organization.

The same is true for respect. The more value you bring, the more respect you will earn. This is amazing. You are in control. Lose the excuses and start digging in. Be the person everybody talks about because of your relentless, unwavering attitude, work ethic, and commitment to excellence.

If you are an employee, give more and do more. If you are a leader, focus on inspiring your people to give more and do more. Get to know what makes them tick. Show them their trajectory. Let them know where they can go with elevated performance. Listen to their needs and deliver on them.

If you are somebody looking to run a championship team or organization, never forget about your people. Your people are everything. Always put your people first.

That is the Torre Rule.

NINE

You're Never Over-Dressed in a Suit.

Being a Pro. I love that word "Pro". Such a simple three letter word, but so much impact. So much respect. One thing I believe we can all benefit from is acting like a Pro.

In today's culture of rapid scrolling, lack of true connection, and noise, a true differentiator is straight up acting professional. Nothing is more impressive than interacting with somebody who does all the little things right.

A strong handshake. Eye contact. Great posture. Well groomed and manicured. Nicely dressed in fitted clothing. A listener more than a talker. A strong and confident voice. All are traits that are truly appreciated. Winning traits. Traits that create confidence in any relationship. If you are just starting out, or are working to test a relationship over time, being a professional makes for a strong foundation.

I know we are taught not to judge others, but the reality is, we judge others all the time based on those traits previously mentioned.. That is the reality. Perception is reality. And, it is ok. It is what it is. So rather than get caught up in debating rhetoric, let's accept that humans will always judge each other. Every first impression, job interview, or interaction has an element of judging. As people, we judge to create and find trust. Once the other person checks all of our boxes, we can open up and judging is "lessened."

For those lacking confidence, the judging continues indefinitely. They judge to create the internal strength they don't have. They judge to give themselves perceived relationship leverage through false confidence. And once again, it is what it is. Accept it. You can hit eject any time you desire. Maintain your composure and never forget, you get what you tolerate. What I have seen behind all true Champions in sports, business, and life is a focus on their approach. They approach all situations with a level of professionalism. Non-biased professionalism. Teaching this to those they lead.

Look at all the great coaches: Lombardi, Coach K, Phil Jackson, Parcells, Torre, Wooden. They teach their players respect and discipline to process. They use certain rules, standards, and values to develop and create excellence—to develop great character and great people. Not only do they expect compliance, they demand it. We achieve excellence over time as we develop professionalism. The result is a lot of winning.

Many people today argue that the way you dress is an expression of character, and you should be able to wear whatever you want, however you want. We are in a free world. Agreed? Y.O.L.O. (you only live once), right?

But when your self-expression hinders the team or organization, that is a problem. If you are a distraction, you are a problem. As a leader, you must address anything or anybody that trumps or tries to trump the overarching organizational and team goal of winning. The "it is not a problem until it is a problem" approach itself is a problem. Never let anything linger or it will perpetuate itself. Guaranteed.

As a leader, set the tone, set the expectation, and demand compliance through your actions. If those under your leadership don't understand your *why*, it is your job to explain it in greater detail. It is your job as a leader to show how A + B = C.

Remember, as we said, everybody is an individual. If somebody has a desire for greater self-expression, show them how they can still be *themselves* while serving the team, rather than over-shadowing the team.

Over the years, many players have come through our organization. Some were louder than others. Some were more eccentric in their dress, but at the end of the day, they respected each other. They respected the manager, the organization, and the big goal of winning championships. Professionalism is such a delicacy these days, but when you can bring professionalism to everything you do, your game will elevate.

In my personal journey, I have worked with elite athletes, CEOs, musicians, and students. The over-achievers were all pros. Even guys that appeared at times to be a bit eccentric were still organized and detailed between the lines. Many of the musicians I know, always say the difference between those who make it and those who don't isn't talent. The difference is being a pro and being able to hold your life together across a forty to fifty-city tour and resisting all the temptation.

Do you crack, or do you rise to the challenge deploying great character, habits, and lifestyle choices? What I always found amazing when working with younger student athletes is that at such an early age you can see who will be a future All-Star and a great future hire. It is as clear as day.

There are always those late bloomers. But to see character and professionalism at such a young age is remarkably impressive and admirable. Because of it, think about the overall marketability of that person. People want to hire them. They want to be led by them. There is more of an incentive to push them into a position of leadership.

Sports, business, and life are not easy, but with professionalism you have the best chance to "make it". Again, this doesn't mean you need to be wound tighter than a snare drum. It just means you need to remember the words of the late, great Joe DiMaggio. As one of the greatest Yankee players of this century, he was asked, "Joe, why do you play so hard every night?"

He smugly answered, "Because I do not know who in the crowd that has not seen me play before. I owe it to them to give it my best effort. That is what they will remember me for. I don't want to let them down."

How do you want to be remembered?

TEN

Failing to Plan = Planning to Fail

**Until the Plan Doesn't Work

There is one man who inspired this chapter. In my daily blog he goes by Riley. In real life he is a true inspiration. Have you ever come across those people that care about what is going on in your life? You know they have a million things going on, but they always take the time to care? That is my friend and long-time client, Barry.

As I trek through life, through thick and thin, Barry is always there to give me advice. What is amazing, is he gives advice on everything! From my route to Manhattan to my flight path to Florida to which rental car company I will use. I told you, "everything".

But the most important lessons he taught me are about planning. Playing *offense* on life. I later realized this was the same philosophy of the late, great Coach John Wooden. Coach spent more time planning his practices than coaching the actual practice. Planning is the key to achieving what you want in life. And, if you fail to plan, you will definitely not get what you want out of life. With planning though, you must also realize that when the plan doesn't work or stops working, it is time to get a new plan! Pivot. Switch the tracks. Change it up!

I would always joke with players that would ask my why they were not hitting. I would always respond with, "Check your bat." The joke was always on them. It is never the bat, unless it is cracked, it is always the guy swinging it. The same is true with plans. Take them seriously. Spend the time designing them. But realize, when they do not work, it is not the plan, unless it is cracked. It is always the designer and plan architect. Full accountability baby! It has been said that success can be broken down into eighty percent psychology and twenty percent strategy. And as we all know, taking care of our headspace as it relates to success should always be number one. A broken head could be the reason behind a perceived broken plan.

When my so-called plans have not worked out, it is not that the plan was necessarily bad, it was that I was not one hundred percent committed to the project. I was half into it. If it works, I would dig in more. If it doesn't, my *not all-in protective mechanism*, or my *told you so* response allowed me the ability to not consider myself a total failure. I gave it my *best* shot. But the truth is this, you gotta be all-in. One hundred percent. Open yourself up to the chances of failure. Feel the heat as it gets ready to burn you. At that point, you have made the decision to crash or burn with whatever it is you are doing.

Dabbling is not a good recipe for winning at anything. All-in is. You can't be half pregnant, and with anything you choose to do, dabbling will allow you to exit when things get tough, rather than rise up and persevere through the hardship that may lie between you and achievement. Create a plan. Get all-in on it, and as the great Michael Jordan said, *attack* with all the juice and ferociousness have in you.

Ok, let's get focused! Back to my man Barry. On a cold February day, he shared with me one of his greatest lessons, "Do what you love in life; that is the only way you will be happy." A true Titan in business and life, Barry has had immense success while keeping his priorities straight. A great husband, a great father, a great CEO, and philanthropist. The list goes on. His greatest asset though is in the wisdom he shares with those he touches, about doing it "your way".

A page out of the book of Old Blue Eyes, Frank Sinatra, you must always do it "Your Way." Nobody can tell you how to *live your life*. Nobody can tell you what your dreams are even though people will try if you give them enough of an opening. Find what makes you tick. Find what you are passionate about and what lights you up. Then, create a plan and attack it with tenacity, confidence, and velocity. Adjust as needed. That is your plan. Believe in it. Own it. Make it happen for yourself.

When we are not priming ourselves up each day, with positive energy and a *can-do* attitude, that opens the space for others to start dictating our dreams, our passions, and their thoughts on what they think we should do. No good. Wake-up every single day, tell yourself this is *my day*, it will be a great day, and I will dominate my plan that is fueled by my passion, mission, vision, and goals. I am a champion. I hold myself to the highest standards. I am relentless. I never quit. I will be victorious on all things I choose to commit my whole self to.

That my friends is positive self-talk. The power of positive self-coaching.

I want to reiterate this since it has been some of the greatest advice I tell myself on a frequent basis. When you create the plan you believe in, stop asking everybody what they think. That is the fastest way to lose your conviction. Own your sh%t. Love it. Believe in it. Through thick or thin! Winning finds the convicted soul and attaches to it.

So, whether you are a CEO setting the plan and direction of your company over the next quarter, a coach looking to win a national championship, or a start-up entrepreneur looking for a profitable first year or product launch, go! Don't ask anybody for permission. Don't ask for opinions. Just go out into the arena and fight for victory.

Set your plan and go. The plan may need adjustments as you get started, but always trust your gut. You may suffer some early bruises and minor losses, it is ok. Keep going. That is all part of the process. Even the best plan will never be perfect. It is impossible to plan everything prior to getting into the ring. If your plan goes ninety percent right you have hit it out of the park.

The first strength coach I ever worked under with the Yankees, Jeff Mangold, would always say, "Dana, always remember, the great ones adjust! Never forget that." Great advice to a nineteen year old trying to be perfect.

How often have you doubted yourself? I know I have. It is scary when you doubt your own plan. Then you get into the question-asking game, waiting on others to validate *your* plan. How could they? It is your plan.

Coaches Tip: Never go against your gut. You are feeling something for a reason. It is your job to identify if it is just fear or an actual core disagreement you are having with yourself and a decision, person, or situation. If it is a core disagreement, and you are thinking of going against yourself, DO NOT DO IT. Never go against yourself no matter how tempting it may be. You will pay royally for it.

Have you ever stopped to think about how ridiculous it is to consult somebody else on your vision, mission, and plan? Advice and coaching are great, but not when it totally neglects your vision. Advice and coaching are great for small critiques and to bounce ideas off of others, but not when it trashes your idea. You must make your own decisions in life. You must own your decisions.

Imagine Elon Musk asking for advice on Tesla, telling people he wanted to create a motor-less car that runs on a computer and is sold in shopping malls. People would think he was nuts. Or, what about the desire to create his own aerospace company so

Americans can enjoy space travel? *Headed to Florida? No, Mars. You?* These ideas are nuts to the average person. They may even seem crazy to other visionaries. But that is what being a visionary is all about. Having vision! What if Elon listened to the critics?

What if Coach John Wooden who never spoke about winning championships asked for advice on his coaching philosophy? Would he have led his team the same way? After all, he became one of the most winning coaches in NCAA history. A true champion.

Innovation is almost always the result of a theory, concept, and plan misunderstood by the majority. It is up to the leader to trust in the plan anyway and find a small group that wants to have a Jerry Maguire moment. You, the fish, and "who's coming with me." All committed to challenging the status quo and doing something remarkably unique.

Do you think we would have understood Henry Ford, JP Morgan, Andrew Carnegie, Cornelius Vanderbilt, Thomas Edison or John D. Rockefeller? Do you think they cared even if we hadn't? Absolutely not. They have confidence and trust in their own abilities and plans. Once they set the plan and took the first step, they became even more aligned to their plan and belief in it. The actuality of achieving what they set out to build became even more real.

With each success and win, buy-in from those initial critics became that much greater. When you have a plan and can combine that with enough conviction, confidence, and naivety, you have the foundation you need to win.

When asked how he built one of the most dominant sports brands of our generation, Kevin Plank, the founder of Under Armour, lived by the saying, "We were always smart enough, to be naïve enough, to not know what we could not accomplish." I mean, this guy had a vision of men wearing sports apparel that was modeled after women's lingerie. But, he was solving a major problem in the process, of wicking sweat off the body onto a fast drying shirt. Amazing. We can't predict the future, so we must get comfortable with the uncomfortable.

We must be ok living at the intersection of trust, naivety, speculation, and risk. On the other side of that is everything you want. In my office at Yankee Stadium, I had the quote on the wall that said, "Get Comfortable with the Uncomfortable."

There was not one day that I pulled up to my office at the stadium feeling comfortable. I knew they could take my job at any moment. I approached everyday like it was my last, and that made it an amazing ride. We all seek security, but the sooner we realize it does not exist, the sooner we will be free to live. Free to explore. Free to challenge ourselves to head into the unknown.

Security is the great myth. Even with a plan, there are no guarantees, just greater chances of staying focused and on a path. Security is a term that in my opinion was a selling a point to those who lived in the 1930s–1980s. Security from a job with a pension allowed you a perfect life on paper. White picket fence, a nice Falcon, three square meals, and a TV set for the family.

Timing was everything. Meaning, after the stock market tanked, people got spooked. Their money disappeared, they became fearful and never wanted to feel that loss again. So, companies sold them on the notion of *security* through a guaranteed monthly wage and a predictable life from now till *the end*. This led to more people valuing a pension rather than the excitement of entrepreneurship and chasing their dreams. Security is an indirect dream killer. Many companies offered people fair or below market wages in exchange for longer work days, benefits, and a pension. And, people took it. Gladly and willingly without question. Most people love predictability. Which is why I feel most people today that are trying to be entrepreneurs probably are not fit for the role. It just doesn't work like that. It is a gig with no guarantees no matter how hard you work, how long you work, and how much you *believe*. Unfortunately, you only succeed if the market validates you by opening up their wallet and paying for your goods or services. Winning in most cases is actually black or white.

Any time you are willing to sacrifice your dreams in exchange for a job (that they can fire you from at any time) you are ultimately sacrificing not just your security, but your freedom and your potential greatness. I am not saying companies are bad or that everybody has to become an entrepreneurial renegade. I am simply saying, wherever you work or put your energy, make sure there is passion there.

Make sure you are giving everything you've got to the entity you serve, whether that be corporate or yourself. If you are on a team or leading a team, give it all you've got. The success of that entity relies on it. You should not interpret this as recommending you to be selfish and all about you, but rather about finding what you love to do, a cause, mission, or company you believe in and going all-in on it. When you find this, the amazing thing is the amount of energy you will have naturally. No coffee, red bull, or five hour energy needed. Just raw internal, self-created horse power to go out and get after it!

My friend and client, Brandon Steiner, CEO of Steiner Sports, gave me a rock years ago that said, "ALL-IN." One of the best gifts a mentor has ever given me outside of their time. From the first time I met him, he told me, "Dana, whatever you do, make sure you are all-in. If you are not, get out."

Think about it, if you are on the fence or skittish, you won't be able to endure the inevitable hardships that go with any career, job, entrepreneurial venture, or appointed position. Do what you love. Do what you are passionate about. Follow your calling in life. When you fall out of love with something, go find what you love and immerse yourself. Trust yourself. Believe in what you are doing. Always have a plan. And remember, when you are just getting started, there is a good chance the money will not be great. But, you are in love with what you are doing. And, because of that, you have your best shot at winning big over the long game. Play the long game.

Remember the words of Barry, "Failing to plan, is planning to fail." Never be afraid to pivot!

Do you have a plan?

ELEVEN

You Gotta Have Moxie

Moxie? What the heck is that? Well, for those of you that are from the New York Area, South Florida, or have seen the movie *Fiddler on the Roof*, you know what moxie is. It is guts. Balls. Chutzpah. Cajones. The only other way you would know is if you came across my mother at any point in your life and spoke about life and business with her.

Barb is a real treat, I will tell you that. A school teacher by day and a fearless ball of jazzercising energy at all times. While growing up, I was always thinking of my next business idea, always looking to push myself forward. Often times though, I didn't have the guts. I didn't have the guts to make the phone call, knock on somebody's door, or go for the interview. This is an issue of putting yourself out there and not worrying about rejection. Rejection is a part of life. Get comfortable with it early.

So, what did my mother do? Every time it snowed, she made my brother and I make flyers the night before and hit every mailbox in the neighborhood. Using our old school printer where you had to peel the sides off of the paper after printing! Talk about time consuming. She made us use the earliest version of Microsoft Word to make the nicest flyer we could to most importantly, get it out there! Fast! I mean talk about time sensitive. If the sun came out, our business was over! Less concerned about how it looked and more concerned with the action. Action. Nothing more important than that.

Snow season was just the start of it! After the snow comes the Spring Clean Ups! More flyers. Then the pool cleaning and lawn mowing service. More flyers. And finally, before the "season" ended, we had leaf raking and fall clean-ups. More flyers. Once we had done the marketing and we got calls, we had to schedule ourselves, do the work, then ask for payment.

Lot's to do for middle schoolers. When we completed the work for others, our father greeted us with twenty yards of mulch every summer in the court we lived in. We had to shovel the mulch into wheelbarrows and cart the mulch across our acre of property until the pile was gone. Grueling. This, combined with cutting the acre of property with a hand mower, will really test you. But when we had done the work, it still wasn't done.

When we *thought* we had completed the work, we would then have to get my dad for his approval. If we missed spots on the lawn, we had to re-cut it in the opposite direction. We had the only yard in the Tri-State area that actually looked like Yankee Stadium. Crisscrossed lines, perfectly straight. If we had to wash the car, there could be no speckles after drying, or we had to rewash.

The way I grew up was typical of kids in the eighties and nineties. "If you are going to do a job, or if someone asks you to do a job, do it right." That was how my father believed we should do work. As close to perfection as possible in all that we do. That was the standard and expectation. So, a combination of intense work ethic and high levels of guts to go get what you want in life, is what makes me who I am today. Tremendous lessons for all. Forget easy. Get to work. Work actually works. Being able to work gives you a tremendous advantage, especially over the coddled silver spooners.

As fear takes over many of us when we are going for a job interview, getting ready for our first at-bat on a new team, getting married, or asking for something we *think* is too big to ask for, remember the following words: "What is the worst they can say? No. And if they do, who cares. Say the word *next* out loud and move on to the next person."

My mother taught me this after I faced some early rejection. It works. It works in life, sales, business, relationships, negative thoughts, you name it. Fear of rejection only exists because you have not been rejected enough. You haven't asked enough tough questions or been in enough big situations.

If you want to succeed at the highest level, you must get rejected. You need to be comfortable with rejection and use it to excite and motivate you to keep going. Rejection is a part of life. What is even more crazy is when you get the greatest acceptance (or YES) of your life from somebody, and years later that same somebody gives you the biggest *rejection* of your life.

That happened to me with my Yankees coaching gig. But, it is a part of the job when you coach in professional sports. When I was nineteen years old, Brian Cashman allowed me to get my feet wet as a young intern with the Yankees. Four years later, he gave me the chance of a lifetime. He made me the Head Strength and Conditioning Coach for the team! Are you kidding me!

An amazing, life changing, opportunity. Leading up to this, I did my best. I worked for free and gave it everything I had. I communicated my thoughts, openly and fearlessly. I worked to come up with innovative ideas and strategies to really make our department (Strength & Conditioning) progressive, and I then marketed these ideas to get buy-in from the players and other members of the coaching and training staff.

It worked. I always approached my department as it's own business within the business.

On a hot April day in Texas, Cash called me into his suite and gave me the greatest opportunity of my life. Phil Hughes was pitching on the mound the night before on a steamy Texas night at the Ball Park at Arlington, and he ended up pulling his hamstring in the seventh inning. I remember it vividly.

Before Cash called me into his suite, which was the biggest hotel room I had ever seen, I was sweating in panic, fearing that my newly appointed job of Assistant Strength Coach would vanish. Instead, he gave me the most amazing promotion. I mean honestly, can you imagine giving a twenty-three-year-old kid the opportunity and responsibility he gave me? That is confidence and belief at the highest level. Also probably a wicked ability to see and project talent, something that would make Cash one of the greatest GMs in MLB history.

As a twenty-three-year-old, I was at the peak of my Professional life. I will be forever grateful to Brian Cashman for making this happen for me. I still think about how it happened to this day. Luck? Maybe. Trust? Had to be. A combination of luck, trust, and my passion? Most likely.

This resulted from putting myself out there and having somebody that believed in me more than I believed in myself at the time, take an educated gamble. I like to think he was right on his gamble. That is why he has been leading the team to victory since the nineties.

But, as we all know, in life, most highs are followed by some lows. About 8 years later, my time with the organization was up. We had been losing, and Brian (who I still respect heavily and dearly to this day) and I parted ways. I was grateful for the opportunity and the new adventures ahead, but rejection always hurts. This rejection was worth it though. In 2009, I became a world champion along with some of the greatest teammates, coaches, and front-office people out there.

Coaching Tip: You must put yourself out there no matter what. Remember, rejection is part of life. We will all experience it if we are taking risks. But, when you get rejected, never become bitter. Always be grateful for the people or organization that at one time gave you acceptance and the word "YES." Be forever loyal to those people. Never bitter, no matter what.

During my time with the team, I learned who I was and most importantly what I was made of. I learned what it took to endure extreme work hours. Extreme travel with time away from home, friends, and family. I learned the art of negotiation. The importance of data, organization, and communication. And, how to deal with some of the biggest names and personalities in sports. What made them tick, what made them great, and how to become a winner in all that you do. I learned to hold myself to an even higher standard of excellence.

As for my career, the positives far outweighed any negatives. I came in as a nineteen-year-old kid with a dream and left a Champion. It is always important to know the game you are playing. Professional sports is a very competitive business. Knowing the game you are playing is half the battle. Once you know the rules of the game and how it works, the outcomes that may happen don't surprise you. They are just part of the game! Get comfortable with the uncomfortable!

There is always growth on the other side of any perceived hardship! Never forget that! Something I learned early in my journey of life was that if you ask, you may get what you ask for. If you don't ask, you will live with regret. That is unacceptable.

Wherever you are in your life, push forward. Onward. Never let a "no" get you down. Turn the "no" into a "yes". You can do this with negotiation, or you can re-frame the circumstances in your mind, so you are a winner! Next! Success is a decision. It is the results of a series of decisions, choices, and experiences. Decide what you want. You just may get it!

And remember, no matter what happens though, when somebody rejects you, they are not rejecting you as a person, just your proposal. And, just because it is a "no" today, does not mean it will be a "no" in the future. Rework your plan. Rework your approach. Rework your product. Then give it another shot. Stay poised, never down for too long. The fighters are the winners. If it were easy, everybody would do it. Very few have championship rings for that reason. Winners are a part of a special club. You can get there.

How about this for tenacity. Kevin Plank, the CEO of Under Armour, made seven-plus renditions of his original shirt before he could make it great. But, that doesn't mean he didn't sell some of his generation ones. His rejections inspired him to chase and create the perfect product, always putting himself out there and selling along the way. Broke, down on his luck, and without enough change to get over the Delaware Memorial Bridge, he caught a break and gave his company new life when a check hit his PO Box. He lived another day and now we get to share in his victory as consumers of his products.

Put yourself out there. Dream big. Have fun in the process. If you are not feeling over-matched slightly, you are not shooting high enough. Cliché, I know. But totally true. Fear is a part of the process. I have fear while writing this book. But, I am doing it anyway. For the one person or one million people it will help.

Coaching Tip: Fear is a part of the process. Everybody is scared. Even the person sitting across from the negotiation table has fear running through them. No matter how intimidating or confident they may look. Remember, Faith Up, Fear Down. Acknowledge it, tip your cap to it, but never succumb to it.

Never let fear dominate you because everybody you meet in life has some. No matter what title they hold or how much money they have, everybody is scared. It comes down to how we deal with it. If you want to be a Champion, you must take the hits. You gotta have moxie.

Do you have the moxie of a Champion?

TWELVE

Find the Bully and Knock Him Out

Have you ever been intimidated by a situation because of your expectations of how things will go? I mean, you are sweating over something that might happen, but has not actually happened. There is a big chance it may not ever happen, but it can still happen.

Get it? Ok, maybe you do, maybe you don't. The point is, no matter how big the situation, or the person you are set to meet with, go in there and knock it out.

One of my favorite clients and friend, Pablo, who is a tremendous success in the world of finance, came to this country not speaking English. Outside of his great accent, incredible athletic ability, six-pack abs, flowing hair, and his suave "can-do" attitude, he had to rely on his grit and gut for survival. His Division 1 Boston College soccer skills were nothing to sneeze at either. Just sayin'.

This was all part of the survival routine he learned when he was a kid in Argentina. He moved around a lot as a kid, forcing him into new schools. We all know how tough it could be to change schools as a kid, the drama of who will befriend the "new kid" and who will look to create dominance and gain territory by being the bully. We are seeing who will be the dog that has to claim territory by lifting the back leg.

One night after a training session, Pablo told me how he earned his stripes in life. It was a powerful story of taking control and owning the room! I assumed he would tell me about some of his persuasion techniques and strategy to gain the trust of the world's business titans and how he gets them to hand over their fortunes. But instead, he told me how he made himself comfortable in his new schools.

"The first day I went to school, I found the bully of the school and punched him square in the eye. That is what you do with the bully. You let him know right away you will not be one of his victims."

Pablo is a nonviolent person. One of the kindest, most generous, and most classy men I know. But this lesson was a big one. After we spoke about the playground, we talked shop about business and situations we find ourselves in. That bully philosophy and action plan can be used any time. When you fear something, knock it out. No matter how big, or how dominant, knock it out.

When you feel hesitant, go knock out whatever you feel hesitant about. If you can train yourself to face the bully which is really another word for fear, head on, your chances of winning and becoming a Champion go way up.

We are all afraid of things. We all have deep rooted bloodlines of fear within us. The only way to get over the fear-hurdles and win the fear olympics is to face your fears. The more fears you face, the greater your outcomes.

Think about it. Face your fears. Even if you want to cry, vomit, or defecate in your pants, just face your fear. On the other side is a stripe and notch on your belt. Fear will kill your dreams. Fear will keep you playing it safe until the day you die.

Another friend of mine runs a mortgage broker-age. He would ask interviewees if they were looking for a secure job? He would follow up and ask them if they desired security over commissions? For those that answered yes, he would reach into his desk and give them an application to the United States Postal Service. After giving them the application, he would firmly let them know he was looking for risk takers willing to put it all on the line. In a job where you typically eat what you kill, security is not a benefit of the job.

He knew immediately that a conservative, security seeking person would not get his company where it needed to be. Therefore, he decided up front to let all security seekers set sail. I always ask my coaching and consulting clients, "If you had a choice of having a secure job, with no elevations outside of three percent annual raise, or a position that might allow you to double your money every twenty-four months indefinitely, which would you take?"

I would preface this with the "double your money" job may send you home empty handed for weeks at a time initially. Their answer would always let me know their risk tolerance. What is interesting about this is that many people are unwilling to take the "double your money" gig but call themselves entrepreneurs, or risk takers. They are entrepreneurs that are actually very fearful. Often times an indication they have had little success yet, or even a sign that maybe solo entrepreneurship is not for them. The better you can self-evaluate, the better off you will be in all you do. Introspection is critical.

These types may be better off becoming intra-preneurs—choosing to be entrepreneurial in the corporate workspace rather than on their own, allowing their creative entrepreneurial spirit to flourish without the fear factor.

For some, because of a low risk tolerance and high fear factor, they may realize entrepreneurship is not their calling. That is just fine! They may be rock stars at something else but are playing the wrong game right now! Sometimes players and people are out of position!

This happens all the time. I have always admired people that have tremendous self-awareness skills and can live in true alignment. They know what they want and aren't influenced by others. They know what they are *here* for and why. Having a very clear understanding of the life they want to live, how much they need to earn to live the life they love, and what the important things are to them. Man, that is so powerful.

These people are great to be around. They are grounded and are usually really easy to communicate with. They seek zero external validation since their sense of self-security is abundant! That is the place we should all strive to get to. A place we should all work to arrive at.

So many are searching today. Living lives filled with discontentment and wonder.

Am I doing the right thing? Am I doing this right? What will so and so think of me? Is this my calling? My passion? I get it. I have been there. We only get one life and we want to be positioned for health, happiness, success, and just flat out winning.

In my coaching business, these folks (the slightly confused and under-performing in some aspect of life, or so they think) usually come to me when they are feeling a lack of confidence, are overwhelmed, have let themselves go, and in extreme cases, are physically dissatisfied with themselves and their performance, or are on the cusp of having some kind of nervous breakdown. Or, some are feeling beat down and have reached their breaking point. Calm down Big Fella!

At this point, they have already subscribed to every marketing, leadership, and self-help program under the sun from live workshops with chain saw juggling midgets at the fountain of youth to online courses that promise you "x" or your money back. Good luck with that!

You name it, they have tried it. Kudos for trying. I always tip my cap to those who are seekers and will do whatever it takes to win for themselves and their families.

I am sorry though, for their financial hardship because of the debt accumulation from engaging in the "get rich quick" circuit. My advice before attending any of these events is to find people that have taken part and see how their situation has transformed because of that particular workshop. Get some data points!

Obviously, not all of these workshops are bad, but before engaging in them, many people fail to realize how the seminar/workshop business actually works. They also fail to realize you can not just attend an event and think you will walk out a success and totally renewed as if it were raining baptismal water. You must be prepared to put in an immense amount of work, applying what you have learned, and also to overcome all those negative patterns and associations that had held you back in life prior to walking through the seminar doors. It takes work to overcome your self.

I learned something very important through some of my personal experiences engaging in some of these courses, workshops, and programs along my journey to success. Most importantly, trust yourself and find people that really care about you as a person. Chances are, you can get free help and mentorship from somebody locally, that has achieved success in the areas you struggle, that enjoys the process of helping somebody else with nothing needed in return. The satisfaction for that person comes from watching you soar. Their payback comes in positive karma and being blessed for their positive deed. People like this do exist. They are just not a sponsored ad on your instagram feed.

As my client, Daniel, always says, be very careful of low-barrier-to-entry businesses and the personalities in them. These types of businesses are a perfect breeding ground for scammers, smooth-talkers, and your typical snake-oil salesman-types—promising the world, delivering on nothing.

When I end up coaching people who have been "taken" or are struggling to find success and clarity in sports, coaching, business, life, or their career, my earliest steps always involve a complete intake evaluation, followed by reworking their health and personal performance plan, then reworking their life and lifestyle plan.

Why do I start there? It is an atypical place to start but let me share with you my *why*.

The process of success and finding "your true self" is grueling and can be very abusive on the mind and body. This often leaves the body and mind somewhat depleted, deprived, and beat-up. We have to get that mind-body connection working again! Fired up. Excited. Feeling great. During the process of physical and mental re-firing, people gain more confidence and self-belief. Two things that are often the first to go during times of stress and anxiety. These are the foundational components of success and personal satisfaction. Increase personal confidence and self-belief and anything is possible. That is the first important shift in the transformation process. A healthy body and a healthy mind allow this process to happen much easier. Whether you are an athlete, a coach, or a business person, in order to excel, you need a strong mind and body as your foundational building blocks. Then you can worry about strategy and skill.

Let me give you an example: Have you ever seen a person, male or female, that has been recently divorced? After the grieving phase, they go into the "clean-my-fat-a$$ up" phase. One year after their divorce they look fabulous. Mojo is high. Moxey is strong! Confidence is rocking! Anything is possible! They exercise to improve their marketability and chances for success. It is an amazing innate human response how the psyche of a person knows that in order to achieve success, the dead weight must be shed, and as a result, the confidence mindset is rebuilt and retooled for better *performance*. These people are like a car that has been in the garage for twenty years rusting out with dust and webs and now have to head to a Barrett-Jackson Car Auction.

What happened? They cleaned up the physical to advance their mental confidence and state. Their mindset went from that of passive to aggressive. Many struggle because they are out of alignment. Who they are, their current results, and what they want or their values are not in line. With the above process we are realigning them from the inside out. Matching their internal health, mindset, and compass to that of a high performer. This sets them up so their internal environment is ready to handle the high performance demands, and championship outcomes they desire.

Many individuals are so blocked physically and mentally they couldn't see the road to success if they were already on it! As we work to develop a newfound mission, vision, and goals, what we also discover through the coaching process is that many of these future Champions were chasing the wrong thing or things. Things that were actually bankrupting them mentally, physically, and spiritually, exhausting them and their spirit. Leaving them totally smoked.

They were being "posers," as I like to call them. Frauds. Fakers to themselves. Tricking themselves into believing what they were doing was right, or what they were "supposed" to be doing. The findings of interrogative coaching show that what they thought they wanted, was not what they actually wanted at all. And, what is often uncovered is that what they were doing was not what they are destined to be great at.

Imagine how exhausting it can be on you mentally and physically being and doing something you think you are supposed to be doing but have no passion or mission for it?

Look at it like this. Many people think they want to run or build a Fortune 500 Company and that will be the answer to all their problems. Riches will solve all their problems. But the reality is they are just looking for a feeling of safety and financial stability. They may also crave the feeling of a position of leadership. The desire to tell others what to do. Many want to be leaders because it makes them feel powerful, relevant, and important. Their passion is not actually to lead or build a great company, but they feel these feats will be the answer to their own internal conflicts.

Coaching Tip: If you have internal conflict, no position, title, amount of money, material things, or status elevation will ever bring you the feeling of peace, calm, stability, and comfort. In fact, a higher position, a better title, more money, and elevated status can cause you more pain because you have not addressed the underlying foundational cracks! Externals can never solve an internal problem. Rebuild yourself from the inside out.

Meanwhile, no title can ever help you conquer your internal demons. In fact, even if you get the position or title, those untamed little rascal demons may cause you even greater problems. They need to be handled and corrected, not masked by title, position, or the building of a corporate behemoth.

We all want to be rich in some way. Many of us think wealth is measured in dollars and cents. Your measurement system of wealth is usually derived from how it was measured by your parents, or those you spent the most time with growing up. This puts many people in the wrong position on the field. They are working jobs and doing things they don't enjoy or have a passion for. They are "out of position." In life, when you are out of position, you can make bad decisions professionally and personally, increasing your chances of losing, not winning.

Imagine a quarterback trying to kick field goals, or a pitcher trying to do anything but pitch (especially lefties-very one-dimensional players!). Here is one for you, a doctor or foreign language teacher coaching linebackers how to tackle. Get in the right position for success. Another thing I have learned through the years, is that not everybody is meant to be monetarily wealthy. Sorry everyone. Some people will be wealthy in knowledge, in skill, in relationships, in influence, but will not be huge earners. That is ok. Accept it and be great at what you are meant to be great at. Your best chances for victory will align to that anyway. So do it with passion. Give it all you got. The results will take care of themselves.

The truth is this, many are doing what they do for status and they think it is what they are supposed to be doing. Rather, they should do what they love or want to be doing because that is most likely their calling. It is an epidemic. People are settling. People are taking risks in the wrong places. People working jobs and running companies they absolutely despise. As a result, they are in pain. I had no idea I would be an author. I hated reading as a kid, but always loved to write and create. So, rather than resist, I dug in!

To get somebody to thrive, the goal is to create alignment in the three key areas of our existence. Life. Business. Health.

Life includes our relationships, our family, our values, and our experiences. Business includes what we do to earn a wage and grow ourselves financially and professionally every day. The company or team we run, or the company or team we work/play for.

Our health includes our physical and mental state. Healthy body. Healthy, vibrant, creative mind. High energy, creative, youthful soul filled with optimism and appreciation. We break down each category to discover where you are thriving (physically, emotionally, professionally, and spiritually), and where you are dying (physically, emotionally, professionally, and spiritually).

I know many people that run billion-dollar companies that are miserable with eroding health and a terrible home life. They are horrible to be around. These are people that never got help, and instead opted for a death spiral in all areas of life but their wealth management portfolio. They fell in love with the cash game and out of love with themselves and everybody else around them. Lonely, miserable, soul-less bastards. Is that success? Is that being a Champion? Is that being a positive influence on those around you? No way.

Non-Champion like Habits performed over a long time have brought them to this place. I am in the business of building Champions. Championship behavior and alignment is what I am all about. Seeing people in this state, or on their way is gut wrenching. Especially since the process can stop at any time with a *decision* to stop it. The power of choice. As a young man, I thought if you were rich, you were a winner.

Then I met some rich people. Really, really rich people. I realized quickly these were not winners, but losers. They won at Chase and Bank of America but lost at home. They lost at the doctor's office. They lost on the scale. They lost with their relationships and with their children. They lost where it mattered most.

That is not winning. These were also some of the biggest cowards I have ever met. The bullies at school. The problem is, nobody ever had the confidence to knock them out and Pablo-ize them. What makes me a Champion every day is having the grit to face my own demons and let others know I am battling. Every single day, I face my fears and annihilate them. So should you. That is a Champions mentality. That is a Champion Habit.

So, the next time something scares you, don't run. Don't stop in your tracks and melt. Take a deep breath and visualize yourself as victorious. Run right through it.

And, sometimes, facing a demon is walking away from something or somebody you love, think you love, or once loved. If something or somebody stops serving you the way you need and does not align with your character or values, walk away. No need to explain. Face your fears with yourself and keep moving. Next.

Remember this; The only person that can stop you is you. Dominate your fear. You will, at times, have to dominate yourself and tame your own mind like a wild elephant. You can do it. If you believe you can, or you believe you can't, either way you are right!

Now as we complete this chapter, let's all commit to going hard after that "big bully" in our life. Fear nothing but fear itself. Your dreams matter. Make them a reality. Get in the right position. Align yourself. Don't leave your music inside you.

Let's take action together, right now. And Knock It Out.

THIRTEEN

Pace Yourself. If You are Going to Eat, Make Sure You Digest.

Growing up with an Italian grandmother, she taught us how to eat. Clean the plate. Use a piece of bread to Zamboni whatever sauces were left in the dish. The bread, was not only the fourth utensil, next to the fork, spoon, and knife, but it also became an extension of the dishwasher. For my paisanos out there, you know what I mean. Forza Italia!

The rule was, as soon as you finish your first helping, there was a second helping waiting and ready to go. What is amazing, though, is how what you learn at the table can translate over into your sports and business life. More. More. More. One plate is never enough. No matter how full your plate, there is always room for another portion and for coffee and cannolis.

Translation: No matter how busy you are, no matter how much you have going on, there is always room for more. Make the time. Fill your plate. Just don't spill, or at least try not to!

For Coach Dana Cavalea, like many high performing Type A ragers; down-time, silence, rest, and doing nothing were never an option. Those are the four scariest states to be in for a Type A overachiever to live in. These states become the breeding ground of immense panic and the sensation of *falling behind* or losing ground to the self and competitors. Most of the time, this is only happening in our own mind.

Years ago, I built a franchise brand of small athletic training studios in New York. They were exact replicas of the facility I had built inside Yankee Stadium. Our tagline was "train like a pro". With that tagline, great locations, and a killer look, I thought we would be unstoppable. Destined for success. Franchises across the globe! Investors lining up to pad my pockets and ego. Can you say "Forbes 40 under 40!" Cohiba cigars in the Caribbean in no time! Not so simple pal.

After having our first facility go profitable in just the first few months of business, we played that hand for the next several years, winning month over month. Easy peasy! So, if you build one that is successful, what is your next move? Build another, obviously. And another. And another. And another.

My philosophy was simple. If one facility was doing great, so would the others. If you can run two facilities, you can run four facilities. And now for the greatest philosophy of all, "If you build it, they will come," . . . until they don't.

I learned very quickly that the health and fitness industry runs in three to five year cycles. Concepts are hot, then they are not. Every three to five years, the next best craze hits the neighborhood and you become old news, no matter what your tagline or claim to fame is. About six years into this fitness brand experiment, I was experiencing the strongest emotion of all. Failure.

We were hemorrhaging money, taking from Peter to pay Paul just to keep our most successful shop open. Employees were stealing money, clients, and contracts, trading in their character for dead presidents. What was once a scalable dream filled with optimism and the desire to change as many lives of possible was becoming a vortex of fiery, confidence killing hell. Me and my team were fighting every day to keep the operation going.

Emotional State = Pissed Off

This was the equivalent of sitting at the table, eating and eating, and having the worst reflux of your life. I was dealing with *professional reflux* in the form of stomach clenching, throat closing, fear, anxiety, twenty-four seven strategizing on how to stop the bleeding and head-pounding mental ping pong searching for solutions.

When you know a ship is sinking, you feel like your luck is so bad you want to make sure the lifejacket you grab doesn't have a hole in it! The focus becomes "easing the pain of loss" and protecting yourself (your ego, your self-worth, your winning track record, your image as a local hero and public figure.)

This state of mind typically arrives after you blame the holiday season, the winter, the school breaks, and any other reason you can find, as to why people are no longer coming through our doors? This situation was so bad I even sent the master himself an email, Marcus Lemonis AKA The Profit. Let's see what you can do with this Titanic of a business Marcus! He never called, so I was left to trust my own instincts.

Not that I have been divorced, but I am guessing the feeling is similar. What you once loved is now slowly killing you. And as my circumstances in life and business were changing daily, I remember what one of my clients told me when I was filled with jet fuel, embarking on the journey of a lifetime to build the next great fitness empire at rocket like speed.

"Dana, how is that business of yours going?"

"Daniel, it is going great! We are making money, people love the concept, and I am going to build three more with the profits from the first one!"

Coaching Tip: Pace yourself. More is not always better. In most cases, it is not. Make one thing great. As hard as it is to stay focused, patient, and consistent, remember this is the formula for success in all you do. Slow down to speed up.

"That is great. But just remember, in business, you can't be eating all the time. Take the time to digest. Sometimes digestion can take years. Be patient, or you will start to over-eat. I have made all of my money on overeaters as they are throwing up at the table."

Great advice that was not taken by yours truly. I preferred my "I'll show you" attitude. He obviously didn't realize who I was and my capabilities. To this day that is the best advice I didn't listen to. He also told me, "Dana, if you are ever at the negotiation table and you do not know who the schmuck is in the room, it is probably you. Every room has a schmuck." The reality is, I made the same mistakes years earlier in baseball and real estate.

"Hi, I am Dana Cavalea, the schmuck in the room."

As a player, I practiced and played all the time. That led to fatigue, breakdown, and injury because I never recovered. I was always beating myself up, never allowing time for recovery. Luckily, while coaching the Yankees, I didn't push my negative habits of obsessive work onto the players. I made sure rest and recovery was the foundation of our training program. Digestion.

When I was in college, I wanted to become a real estate investor. Always being passionately persuasive, I convinced my dad to put some (most) of his retirement into an investment property in the Tampa Bay Area.

We bought one. Rented it. Easy-peasy (you know where I am going with this). Then, we bought another. And another. And another. Things were going great until our tenants destroyed our homes and the real estate bubble burst. Once again, what started out as an empire in the making, very quickly started to erode. We had to pull the ripcord. After years of negotiating with banks, we got out.

There is a pattern here. Too much eating, not enough digestion. Slow and steady is not sexy, but it works in all that you do. Power of focus. Sometimes fear and panic are masked in speed and quantity of creation and acquisition, never giving anything the true maturation period it needs to grow big and strong. They key to life though, is to keep moving forward, not discouraged, not fearful, but smarter. Understanding the patterns. Your patterns and the consequences of those patterns. Life is about patterns.

Our circumstances and results in life are the result of our daily habits and patterns. We are all going to make mistakes. You become a real schmuck if you make the same mistakes repeatedly. If your sales pitch continues to fail, are you going to keep using it and blame the prospective client or market for the fail?

If you keep gaining weight, are you going to blame the restaurants where you eat? If your team keeps losing are you going to keep blaming your team? Study your habits. Study your results. Look at yourself and your actions from a bird's-eye view and you will be able to evaluate yourself without bias. Maybe you still can't give yourself a non-defensive evaluation. That is ok. Hire a coach.

Maybe you need to fail more to wake up. Many of my coaching clients have been floundering for years before we work together, unable to take action and get the results they want. That is when you need a coach—an outside party commissioned to get you on track. A person who knows what you are going through, understands your habits and patterns, and can get you back into the flow from a physical, business, and life standpoint.

The key is listening. I had a great coach but chose not to listen. Coaching and mentorship are amazing. Napoleon Hill documented and highlighted the power of mastermind groups and meetings dating back to the times of Andrew Carnegie and John D. Rockefeller. If some of the most brilliant people in American history were able to benefit from coaching and masterminds, why would you think you could or should go at it alone? Take my advice, it is a bad idea to lead a one man army into war.

Coaching Tip: Find a coach, start or join a mastermind group. Do something. Get in the room with people that can shoot you straight, not for their best interests, but yours.

So, the next time you take a seat at the table of business and life, remember portion control and the importance of digestion. More is not always better. Play the long game and prepare to win over time. If you are going to eat, make sure you digest.

Thanks Daniel. -From All of Us.

FOURTEEN

Don't Tell Me, Show Me.

Have you ever met a person who just keeps telling you what they are going to do, but does nothing they say they will do? This is a major problem. Unintentional chatter is what I call this. Bullsh%t. Or, in sports, we call this *eye wash* and *lip service*. Take your pick. It has no value and is a complete waste of time.

Is the person spewing this chatter trying to waste your time? No. They are sharing their *perfect world* situation and goals with you. They are sharing their dreams with you. But, dreams without action are just fantasies or a pipe dream, and really annoying to listen to when you know that no action will follow.

Don't waste your dreams, kids. As Sonny from *A Bronx Tale* says, "There is nothing worse than a waste of talent." As a kid, I remember telling my dad all the things I was going to do. He always met these fantasies, goals, and potential realities with the bold saying,

"Don't tell me, show me. Anybody can talk. If you do enough doing, other people will start doing the talking for you."

Now, as a kid, when your parent, who is supposed to be your biggest cheerleader, greets your plans with these harsh remarks, the first thought is, "I will show you, jerk." I felt that way until I understood what he was talking about. As we run through life, we meet all kinds of people. Talkers. Do-ers. Winners. Champions.

The talkers, I have found, are the most entertaining. They are full of stories, captivating bravado, inspiration, motivation, an incredible Instagram page, and "look at me" moments—followed by epic disappointment. Big-time highs and bone-chilling lows. One million followers today, dead broke shaking a can on a corner five years later.

The talkers seem to always let you down. Since they are always talking, often forgetting what they are even saying. They forget the things they commit to while talking, and even the things they promise they will do or get for you. Forgive them. They talk often times out of nervousness and make themselves feel good by promising the world, or telling you who they know. It is all based on insecurity, so don't think to deeply about it or take anything they say personal.

Talkers are the worst. They suck. The sooner you recognize a talker, the sooner you should realize they are entertaining and are fun to laugh at, but their words are like beach erosion. Here today, gone tomorrow. A quick hitting storm. Hurricane Irma type damage. No regard for the devastation.

Again, not that these are bad people, but they just are not a fan of what I call, "The Do." They would rather talk about what needs to get done, and should be done, but will not get it done unless it absolutely serves them 100 percent. They are selfish bastards that are working their own agenda 24-7.

In baseball, we often say, "Don't talk about it, Be about it". A trendy way of saying, "Shut up and get it done. Whatever it takes." So after all of those car rides home from games with my dad, the message has now become loud and clear. Say what you mean. Mean what you say. Get it done and shut your mouth. If you commit to something, see it all the way through.

Hard words for the times we are in. But in a land of self promotion and narcissism, this becomes the fastest screening process around to know if somebody is full of it, or a real person of their word. Authenticity. Integrity. Values Focused. Loyalty. That is my kind of person. What type of people do you find yourself with? Do you see any themes?

For years, I was attracted and captivated by the "talker." I found everybody else to be somewhat sterile. When you get let down enough, you realize those *sterile* folks are often the real deal. Process driven, working at their pace, diligent, detail oriented, and present enough to take in and understand everything coming at them.

This reminds me of one of my favorite Denzel Washington quotes from the movie *American Gangster*, "The loudest in the room is usually the weakest in the room." So true. Weakest can also stand for most insecure, scared, and often most out of touch with their personal realities and deep, subconscious emotional state. Again, not bad people, just always staring at their own mirror giving themselves showers of self glorifying empty love.

Whether you are on a team and have a blabbing teammate, or in a workplace with a co-worker or boss that is a false-promiser, know your surroundings. React accordingly. I have found that once I understand who somebody is, and what they are about, I can optimize the way I work with them, should I even choose too.

Once I understand them and what they are all about, I can then identify their skill sets that have value or how to position them effectively on the team and around me should I see fit.

Example: If you have somebody on the team that is highly entertaining, a talker, and a master of ceremonies, they may be great to send out to lunch meetings to get new business. The important thing though, is to send somebody with them who can record the meeting, take notes, and make sure you can deliver the promises they mentioned can and will be delivered upon.

This is an effective way of building a team. If every basketball team had five Michael Jordans, they would probably struggle since those players that surrounded Jordan helped him achieve personal and team greatness. Without Pippen and Rodman, would MJ be MJ?

So often, we are quick to label and dismiss people instead of identifying their strengths. Everybody has weaknesses and they are often glaring, especially to the Type-A leader. But, remember that everybody has strengths as well.

Another piece of advice from my father goes something like this. Put people in a position of strength. This will help them succeed, which in turn, will help you succeed. That is great leadership. Brilliant. Not bad for a musician and teacher. Just kidding pop. My dad was a world class musical conductor getting the most out all the young musicians he worked with and developed.

His forte was teaching his students and proteges not how to eat, but how to fish. What do I mean? The goal was to develop musicians that can read music, understand music, and not just learn the music for the concert or test.

After speaking with him about his teaching career at a deeper level, he never intended to just teach them music. His ultimate quest was always to develop them as people through his passion and love for music. Music was the gateway to their soul. Music created the environment for personal development and growth of humanity. Deep, I know. But, amazing. You can do the same.

How many of you are leading organizations and teams but are feeding your people without teaching them anything? Or worse, leading them without growing and inspiring them. Maybe you are pissed off they don't listen to you. Maybe they don't trust you. Or, they don't think you have their best interest in mind. Or, you are cheap and not paying them what they are worth. Or, they feel that you don't value them. Whatever it may be, I don't know. But one thing I know for sure is this; don't waste the opportunities leadership brings to make an impact and change the lives of those you lead for the better.

If you lead, you must teach. It is your job to build culture daily and make sure all of your "students" understand the goal and mission of the entity they serve. If they don't, how can you possibly be upset with losses? You were working with an unqualified team. You can't expect a single A, minor league team to beat a major league team, right? Teams need to practice. Skills need to be developed. People need to be directed and led. Stop being lazy as a leader and go pull the greatness out of those who serve you, your company, your organization, and, or team. Laziness is another loser habit, not a champion habit.

Coaching Tip: What if we train and develop our people and they leave? What if we don't and they stay? A powerful set of questions. Invest in your people. Lead them. Believe in them. Inspire them. Their growth will reflect in their work and results. Never assume those you lead just *know what to do. Chances are they don't.*

So, no matter what the team is that you are a part of or lead, give it all you've got. Set the tone. Set the expectation. Learn what makes each individual *tick*. The human spirit is amazing when it is activated and launched into battle. It is amazing what people are capable of.

Even the guy that sits in the corner, introverted, and who is considered by many to be weird, can often be the guy that "gets it" and rises with the tide. Let's all commit to leading with our actions, rather than just our mouth. When you are questioning yourself in your role as a leader, remember the words of Big Joe Cavalea, "Don't Tell Me, Show Me."

Results are all that matter. It starts and ends with people. But it always starts with you.

FIFTEEN

Sometimes You Have to Go Backwards to Move Forward.

And, sometimes you have to slow down to speed up. I actually thought life was easy. Yup. I mean, outside of a few tests in high school, and the anticipation and fear of going away to college, things were in sequence, linear, and simple.

Being a huge Yankees fan growing up, my dream was to get onto the field at Yankee Stadium, in the Bronx, New York. My decision to go to school at the University of South Florida put me that much closer to the Bronx, believe it or not. Power of choice. Who would have thought traveling 1500 miles from the Bronx would put me that much closer!

The Yankees held spring training in Tampa every February. I was in Tampa. Therefore, all I would have to do is get a job or internship there, and boom! Off to the house that Ruth and Jeter built.

And it worked! I studied hard in school, networked with the right people, and worked my a$$ off, which gave me the opportunity of a lifetime. Perfectly scripted. Just like the books say. Have a clear target. Prepare yourself. Visualize. Activate. All of your dreams will come true.

That was my life. A damn fantasy. The biggest tease in the world. It was all sunshine and rainbows until I left Brian Cashman, the General Manager's, office on a cold day back in December 2014, when he told me we were going our separate ways.

Who was I at this point? Thirty-one years old. Unemployed. My prime was behind me. Shattered inside but a face of rock on the outside. Nothing lasts forever. I was now, Dana Cavalea, the former Head Strength Coach & Director of Performance for the Yankees.

Former = *A former somebody.*

Like that, it was over. From that day looking through the fence in Tampa, snapping pictures with my flip phone, of all the players, filled with dreams of one day touching the field, achieving that goal, and boom! I was back on that side of the fence.

So far away from the expansive hotel suite in Texas when I got my life-changing promotion. Feeling alone, like a failure, that I could have done more, and the fear of *what am I going to do now.* The next few years would be the biggest test I ever had to face.

Before I walked out of Yankee Stadium on that cold winter day with the final box of *stuff* from my office under my arm, I wrote a note for my unnamed predecessor that said, *"Use this position to do great things for all of those you get to touch and work with."*

I knew deep down I had done that. That I was sure of. That was my purpose in life. To help people find and achieve their personal greatness in life. As the final curtain closed that day, which was a steel garage door to the player's parking lot under Yankee Stadium, letting me out into the open road, the chapter was over. Memories were all I had left. Having my name called over the stadium sound system before opening day in 2007, the smell of champagne drenched carpets from all of our playoff celebrations, and those daily interactions and laughs that came from working alongside some of the funniest, biggest kids, known as professional ballplayers.

Thank you.

Forever blessed.

I fielded phone calls over the next few days from the media and all of my players. An amazing outpouring of care and support, gratitude and appreciation. True friendships that would never die. Deep down, I knew it was a curtain that would never fully close because we had done so much behind it. Winning championships. Changing lives. Battling through sickness and health. That was what I was a part of. A great story it was. I could not have scripted it any better. Ever year, a new group of men that would meet up every February, and battle through October chasing their childhood dream of winning a championship. Amazing.

Hitting the open road that day was the road to *freedom*. Heading home. Going back to where it all began for me. Training the youth of today, the future pros of tomorrow. Taking my skills and experiences and sharing them with next generation. More impact. I thought it would be enough. I thought I could close the Yankee chapter quickly and move on, unscathed. Life doesn't work that way. Life until this point was too easy for me. Everything came too easy. I was not immortal. Not immune to the pain of loss. Not immune to the semi-depressive state the follows massive career and life change. Especially when that career was your dream and all you knew since you were a nineteen year old dreamer

The Big Guy upstairs was not going to just *allow me* to move on to my next venture without me paying my dues. Over the months that followed, I exited a long-term toxic relationship, would have to settle debts on my failed sports training business, and finally, the hardest thing of all, had to battle all the anxiety and negative thoughts that tried to break me.

Break me? Never. Nothing would kill me. Certainly not my own mind. I spent my whole life taking risks, was filled with piss and vinegar, ready to take on the world every single day with guts and vigor. But for the first time, I experienced the phrase, "I can't." I had no energy, no ambition, and felt a bit lost.

Slightly depressed, I ended up moving back in with my folks, back to my hometown for what felt like a decade, even though it was only about six months. This move was not because of financial hardship or suicide watch, but I knew if I wanted to move myself forward, I needed to go to the most stable place I knew—home. The place where my passion, creativity, and work-ethic was born. Where it would be reborn.

My condo sat vacant, untouched. I had no desire to go back to that place where all my Yankee memories and mental battles lived. The nameplates, photos, jerseys, and gear; all of it. I had to get away. I was mad at everything and everybody. I greeted many people with fake smiles and "I am doing great!" All lies to maintain image and protect my severely battered ego, or what was left of it.

I knew I had to go home. If I was going to get out of this mental abyss alive, I had to go back to where it all started. Spending time with my mother and father. Patrolling the neighborhood that inspired me to greatness. Running on the track that built my physique. Eating at the local restaurants that fueled my soul. My message to myself was simple. Sometimes, you have to go backwards to move forward in life. Sometimes you have to slow down to speed up.

I had to rebuild myself like a last-place sports team with a bad farm system. I was up for the task. I may have been stripped of my title, employment, paycheck, stability and status, but nothing could break my spirit. This would require me to dig deep, but it would get done.

Nothing in life is easy. No matter what battles you face. I met what seemed like my darkest moment on the surface, with great light. A few months into my "resurrection," I met a woman that had tremendous spirit. I was dark, she was light. When the world seemed like it was ending, she showed me how to deal with grief through positivity and mindset. She would become my wife about thirty-six months later. Great choice! It all works out, even when we don't have a plan sometimes.

My mother, the most resilient person I know, was breathing down my back to get my head out of my a$$, like a fire-breathing dragon from Queens, New York. That, met with the balance of my father, who is a master of providing situational perspective. Daily conversations with him over baseball highlights were always focused on moving forward. My dad always says, "Don't dwell on the negative. Just keep moving forward man." And finally, being surrounded by the fearless, thrill seeking, presence of my younger brother, who faces everything head on- no matter what, no excuses.

This was my new team. My *old* team, but my new team. When my world was on fire, this team was a team of Champions that was always there for me. They got me through—got my feet back on the ground. The train was back on the tracks. They got me to realize that we win championships when we believe they can be won. No fear. No doubts. Championship teams are built in the face of adversity. That is where the glory comes from. That teaches you to be grateful for the season. Grateful for the moment. Grateful for life. Grateful to all those who help you through.

My life situation is common. We all lose. It is how we handle losing and how we battle back that makes us true Champions. So, no matter what is happening in your life, no matter how alone you feel, realize the curtain will open again. Every season has first pitch. It is your job to get back in the box and *hit the shit out of it.*

One more thing. Remember this, when your world is "crashing down," don't do anything stupid. Your world is just fine. It may not seem that way at the time, but this too shall pass. It always does. This is my message for you.

Never underestimate your strength.
Gain perspective in all that you face.
It is never as bad as it seems.
Never quit anything but bad thoughts.
Go to sleep tonight, wake up tomorrow,
attack, and repeat.
Tomorrow is a new day. You will have new energy,
new thoughts, and new perspectives.
No matter what you face, twenty-four months later
(or less) you will be renewed if you do the work.
Channel your fire. Use it as fuel to become a steam
engine. Become a Champion. I know it is in you.
Believe it is. Never quit, especially not on yourself.
Fear no storms. Why? You are the storm.

That is what it takes to be a Champion.

Thank you. I love you. Now let's go become Champions together.

Coach Dana Cavalea

BONUS:

A Message from Reggie Jackson You Can't Get There Yet.

Playing against the Boston Red Sox at Fenway is always nothing short of amazing. The history, the tension, the fans, and the games that seemed like they would never end! Four hours. Five hours. Even more when summer rains would come through.

But nothing was better than being in Boston and winning big on a Sunday night, then packing up and taking it back to the Big Apple for a Monday off-day. We were always fortunate when we played the Red Sox, to have Greatness in the Building. Greatness meaning #44. Hall of Famer, Reginald Martinez Jackson. Better known as, Reggie.

To us, he was The Humbler. Walking around the clubhouse, the field, the gym, and the training room humbling people. Nobody got too big when Reggie was around. A quick witted old-timer that would tear you up faster than a pitbull chasing a leg.

Reggie wanted to remind everybody, at all times, of his greatness. That was his schtick. The 1977 three-peat of homers when it mattered most. The showmanship. All of it. Reg was a master of branding and keeping his legend alive.

Some of the greatest humbling moments took place in Fenway, usually around the pistachio tin and garbage pail in the back of the clubhouse, or in the manager's office. One Sunday night in September was my night to be humbled. I figured this would be a good time to share.

Reggie, me, and my buddy Robbie were all sitting in the manager's office talking shop with our fingers crossed we would pick up the big win. It was closing in on midnight, and I saw a beautiful Rolex watch Reggie was wearing.

"Reg, I love that watch," I said. I was then sized-up from head to toe. It was like I woke up a lion.

He gazed at me and said, "Oh yeah? This is a Rolex Daytona. And kid, you can't get there yet."

Wow! Talk about embarrassing, immediately questioning my position in life and in the world of Reggie. He was not done though.

"Yet, is the key word. You can't get there *yet*. Your time will come. Be patient. For now, maybe I can sell you another one in my collection that is a little bit lighter, if you know what I mean."

And that was a very valuable learning lesson for me. Why, you ask? Not because I got knocked on my ass by a Hall of Fame Legend. But, because I learned that life is progressive. We all win at different times. Life is about progression. Where you are today isn't where you will be tomorrow. Your position in life, business, and everything in between is not permanent.

As somebody who has been rushing through life since I learned how to make a buck, I realized that if I keep it up, I will not only be disappointed, but left wondering where my life went. We are always dashing. Sometimes walking is a better way. Reggie let me know that night that anything is possible. Sometimes it is not about your ability, your talent, or your position, but rather your patience.

The ability to endure day after day, week after week, month after month, and year after year is the key to winning the long game. The key to developing and creating a legacy. Too often, we want to win now. But if we win now, we may not be ready handle it, or we may even find ourselves being totally bored, disengaged, and passionless since we no longer have a clear mission, vision, and goal, or anything to go out and work for.

Who would have thought the word "yet" would be so impactful. Three letters that knocked me down and inspired me at the same time. It was the truth. I was not there yet. If you are somebody who finds themselves racing for the finish line, make sure you can take time to pick your head up and breathe during the process. Realize, what you think may be your current dreams, goals, and victories may not be what you are supposed to be doing.

Don't be afraid to pivot. Never be afraid of losing time in life. Life is happening for you, not to you. Never forget that. Some of the greatest moments of your life will come from your "yets". Manage your clock but don't let the clock manage you. Nothing in life is absolute but death. It comes down to what you do in between. Listen to your gut. Use *feel* over stats and analytics. It will never let you down.

In that monumental exchange I had with The Humbler that night in Boston, I personally realized I had more to do in life. I had greater goals than the ones I was currently pursuing. What started as a discussion about a watch became a self-evaluation of my life.

Always take the cues of life and look deep into the mirror. Sometimes, we don't realize we are acting like sheep rather than lions. We think we are just getting sheepish results, not realizing it is because of our actions, self-confidence, and the energy we put out into the world.

So, as you are taking time to evaluate your results, ask yourself, "Am I there *yet?*" Most likely you will realize you have so much more to do. So much further to go. Much bigger things to build and achieve. Don't settle for a Rolex Daytona when you can have the Rolex Presidential.

You have greatness inside of you. It is your job to bring it out. Be real. Be honest. Never Quit.

"You can't get there yet, but you will get there." - #44

Final Words

I hope by now you are feeling like you can take on the world! You can. And if you do, remember what it took to get to this point. Commitment, desire, discipline, focus, and strength.

There will always be battles. No matter how trained your mind is, be ready. Protect the gates to your mind. Control what you can control and resist nothing. As Bruce Lee said, "Be like water my friend," and adapt to the glass and your surroundings.

People will let you down. They will tell you you can't do something. You will tell yourself you are not good enough when you are presented with a challenge or an opportunity. Don't believe it. You are the only one who can stop you. If you wish to climb, you can. If you wish to dominate, you shall.

The standards you set for yourself should be high but fair. Once achieved, they should be reset. As you complete and achieve something, there will always be something else for you to conquer. That is what life is about. That is what Becoming A Champion is about—elevating yourself by constantly putting yourself into situations that are not comfortable. Situations that hurt so bad you want to run, but instead you decide to stay and face the music.

Be there. Live there. Be comfortable in the places most will never dare to go. That is where you will grow. That is where your never ending power will come from. Comfort yields more fear. It presents you with regret at a later time and angst in the present from never taking the risks.

Wherever you are today, do not settle for that place tomorrow. Grow mentally, physically, spiritually, and that daily progress will fill your soul.

Whatever is in your mind, go achieve it. Go. Do not talk about it, just do it. The championships go to the doers. Go do. Action will get you to places you never imagined. Your results will show for the work you put into all you want and desire. It won't be easy. Most times it will not be fun. But, in the end, when you can live with the knowing you did all you could do and you gave it all you had, it will all be worth it. That is the walk of the Champion. That is how Champions are born.

Acknowledgements

Team. That is what it takes to get through life and to WIN in anything that you do. It took an entire team to inspire and motivate me to write this book. I want to take some time to acknowledge and thank the greatest teammates in the world.

To my grandmother- For guiding my steps and for always telling me, "Patience is a virtue." You were right.

To my wife, Lauren- For listening to my daily monologues on life, success, and victory, as well as helping me to conquer any doubts that may pop up! And, for showing me what relaxation looks like! You are an expert!

My Mom & Dad- Mom for the guts and Dad for the work ethic. Love you guys!

Mom & Dad Caglione- Thank you for all the great conversations at the table and backyard! Relaxation at its finest.

My Brother- For fighting and winning the greatest battle any man can face. A true champion, risk taker, and American dreamer.

My Nephews: There are no handouts in life. You eat what you kill. You earn what you work for.

Melina: Go after whatever you want in life. Listen to what is inside of you for guidance in all that you do.

Sisto Serafini "The Doc"- Thank you for our daily calls and helping me through when I needed it most. Love you my brother. Rocco!

Matt Casciano- Thanks for being my business con- sigliere! Who would have thought... and author Jerry.

Korey Goodwin- For telling me that I was a 2 on a 0-10 scale . . . You were right. Life changing advice when somebody can be honest with you. And for always taking the time to listen.

Mike Wickland- Thank you for all our talks over coffee! Thank you for helping me change directions and creating the gold standard of sports performance in Major League Baseball.

Mark Teixiera- For our great conversations every single day. For Cigar Night. For your insights into how to make the game better through training.

Caroline Silva- Thank you for keeping me organized through the years. For your day to day efforts to help me build something great. More to come. Next Chapter.

Eddie & Mark- Best security in the league! Thanks for all the laughs and keeping us safe.

Homer Bush- My first friend and roommate in Major League Baseball. Thanks for showing me the way and taking care of a young guy who was going to be sleeping in his car.

The Clubhouse Staff- Thanks for taking care of me through the years. Your efforts never went un-noticed.

Benny Tuliebitz- Thanks for always being a friend and taking care of "things." Roger Hockenberry- we have had some great experiences! Nobody better to be at IHOP with!

Carl Pavano- For teaching me to take the risk, fear nothing, and to straighten out my tips! #divebomber

Rob Cucuzza- For being a mentor, guide, and the baseball big brother I needed to stay in line! And, for teaching me relationships are *built off the field.* The style advice also helped!

Steve Donohue- For showing me what commitment looks like and keeping me out of trouble! Thanks for all your years of guidance and mentorship. I was proud to be a member of your team. *Hey buddy!*

Brandon Steiner- For the daily conversations on writing a book, speaking, and being all-in. And reminding me that to win in life, YOU GOTTA HAVE BALL$

Gil Chimes-For teaching me the greatest technique in the world to help people live without pain. Thank you for helping this guy learn how to heal the best athletes in the world and for showing me what it looks like to have the best hair in Westchester County.

Chad Bohling- For showing me how to motivate and inspire players without being the loudest guy in the room, but the guy with the ability to always be available, and to understand players at a different level. Drury Inn!

Barry Weisfeld- For teaching me how to see life from 40,000 feet above and for the greatest lesson of all: DO WHAT YOU LOVE IN LIFE, FOLLOW YOUR PASSION AND LIFE WILL BE GREAT!

Daniel Straus- Family first. Business second. Help People. Thanks for reminding me to digest after eating! Your outlook on life has changed mine. Thank you for your friendship, for sharing, and continuing to teach me what success looks like.

Pablo Stalman "PAPA"- For your lessons on how to live, explore, and how to truly appreciate life. You showed me how small the world really is, and how one man can navigate it like he owns it. Love you and Cecilia! Focus on the 10%- And, if you think you can, you can. As for the bullies in life, go after them first!

Lucas Stalman- For teaching *me* how to dream again and showing me what it looks like to chase a dream. One of the best young Coaches I have ever had! A true champion as a man and ballplayer- even at 6:00 a.m.! I am excited to see what the future brings for you! Dale'!

Kevin Plank- For teaching me what business really is: A Story. With a clear beginning, middle, and end. I have been watching your leadership for years from up close and afar. Thanks for showing me how to win as the underdog and for letting me be a small part of UA. #protectthishouse

Coach Ron McKeefery- Thank you for showing me how to lead others by focusing on the little things. The little things are what make coaches great!

Jeff Mangold- Thank you for giving me the chance to be your Assistant and cut my teeth in MLB. The great ones adjust!

Joe Torre and Joe Girardi- The only two managers I have ever worked under. Thank you for showing me that two different leadership styles can still yield success. Thank you for allowing me the opportunity to go into battle with you. Joey G- thank you for being the best workout partner I have ever had!

Derek Jeter- For showing me what is means to be a Champion and to be a true professional. For the lesson in a cold Detroit training room one day, where you reminded me defensiveness is really a mask of insecurity. Thank you for giving me the opportunity to coach you.

Jorge Posada- For giving me a shot to take care of you and giving me the right of passage in the Yankees Clubhouse. You gave me the confidence I needed to do my job. Thanks for being a great friend and showing your trust in me.

Andy Pettitte- For dining with me every meal and showing me how to compete daily with consistency. For teaching me to focus on my character and my reputation will be taken care of via a vertical relationship. And, for our shared passion of chocolate chip pancakes!

Mariano Rivera- for teaching me that life and how we handle it is all in our own mind. Slow down. Quiet the noise. One pitch at a time.

Alex Rodriguez- for being a friend, teammate, and role model on how to deal with adversity and overcome anything that comes your way. For showing me the power of relationships.

Steve Sclafani- for all the time you made for me, helping me develop as a young business man. Your time was so very much valued. Our friendship even more.

Jon Gordon- Thank you for your mentorship and introduction to the world of authorship! We all need a rabbi in life!

George McGovern- Your words on Sundays were always music to my ears. Although I did not say much, I always listened.

Ryan Lee- for your daily inspiration via the world of business and marketing!

Kevin Wilson- Love it or Shove it! Thank you for your inspiration and your words. There is no greater lesson than staying true to who you are and who you serve. Hitting is simple, it's just not that easy.

Michael Boyle- For your endless commitment to telling the truth and training/ developing the coaches of tomorrow. Thanks for all your time, words, and teachings!

Dan Gray- For your endless passion to development, your words of encouragement, and your passion for the game of baseball. You are a first class person and coach!

Adam Elberg- for our annual meetings (usually at the lunch table) and for showing me what true leadership looks like. Leave nobody behind. Never compromise your character, your beliefs, and what you stand for.

Lisa Curtis- my personal mental coach! For years of support and pushing me to never be comfortable and never allowing me to make excuses! You rock!

To all the great athletes I have been fortunate enough to coach and impact over the years. Thank you for trusting me with your greatest asset. You.

And finally, Brian Cashman- For giving me the greatest shot of my life. Thank you for believing in me and allowing me to learn from you. Perception is reality.

SPEAKING

Coach Dana Cavalea delivers **keynote speeches, team building workshops, and motivational talks** to companies, athletic teams, universities, athletic departments, and organizations across the country, designed to motivate, inspire, and encourage all those in attendance to become Champions of their own life.

Visit danacavalea.com to book Coach Dana Cavalea to speak at your next event!

JOIN COACH DANA CAVALEA'S
#TRAINLIKEAPRO DAILY BLOG TODAY
AT WWW.DANACAVALEA.COM

JOIN SOME OF AMERICA'S TOP
ATHLETES, COACHES, AND CEO'S ON
THE BLOG AND GET DAILY CHAMPION
HABITS SENT TO YOUR EMAIL!

Follow Coach

Instagram @therealcoachd

Twitter @danacavalea

LinkedIn @danacavalea

MVP 1 ON 1 COACHING WITH COACH DANA CAVALEA

Did you enjoy Habits of a Champion? Are you looking to take your own life and game to the next level? Through 1 on 1 MVP Coaching, Coach Dana Cavalea works with you to help you optimize your performance physically and mentally so you can become a champion in all that you do.

Visit danacavalea.com and click *coaching* to schedule your personalized strategy session. A $299 value, free, for Habits of a Champion readers.

About The Author, Coach Dana Cavalea

Dana Cavalea spent 12 years with the New York Yankees Organization, many of those years as the Director of Strength and Conditioning & Performance Enhancement winning a World Series in 2009.

In addition, he was the recipient of the 2009 MLB Nolan Ryan Award. This award is given to MLB's top Strength Coach as voted by his peers. During his career, Dana has had the opportunity to train greats such as Alex Rodriguez, Derek Jeter, Mariano Rivera, Andy Pettitte, Justin Verlander, and more.

"My objectives are to bring the same techniques, culture, attitude, service, first class training and development programs to Entrepreneurs, Executives, Companies, Students, and Pro Athletes.- Coach Dana Cavalea

Currently he is a high performance speaker and consultant to Pro Athletes, Entrepreneurs, Business Executives, Workforces and Universities on lifestyle strategies to reduce stress, improve work/life balance, and most importantly improve daily performance/outcomes. All of this is known as Performance Enhancement.

Dana has formulated plans and strategies to improve sleep, reduce pain, lower stress, improve body composition, speed-strength-power, as well as mindset training for maximal performance.